NORTH CAROLINA
STATE BOARD OF COMMUNITY COLLEGES
LIBRARIES
ISOTHERMAL COMMUNITY COLLEGE

ISOTHERMAL COMMUNITY COLLEGE LIBRARY
SPINDALE. N. C. 28160

OLD TRYON ROOM

X T

NORTH CAROLINA
STATE BOARD OF COMMUNITY COLLEGES
LIBRARIES
ISOTHERMAL COMMUNITY COLLEGE

OLD TRYON ROOM

CHOO CHOO
The Charlie Justice Story

*Best Wishes and Im
proud to be on Display in
this great room —
Charlie Choo Choo Justice*

CHOO CHOO

THE CHARLIE JUSTICE STORY......

by **Bob Quincy** and **Julian Scheer**
illustrations by **Lee Kolbe**

Foreword By W. D. CARMICHAEL, JR.

BENTLEY PUBLISHING COMPANY — CHAPEL HILL, N. C.
1958

FOR EDITH AND GINNY

COPYRIGHT 1953 BY JULIAN SCHEER AND BOB QUINCY

PRINTED IN THE UNITED STATES OF AMERICA

* * * * *

Library of Congress Catalog Card Number 58-59827

* * * * *

FIRST EDITION

27,963
us

A FOREWORD

Since the earliest days of civilization "numbers" have held special significances in the lives of mankind.

The number 1 signifies God—primacy, the first, the topmost, the utmost. Number 2—a pair of lovers, shoes, stockings, or cups of coffee. Number 3 signifies the Trinity. The numbers 4, 5, 6, 9, and 11 are athletic team symbols. The number 7 means the dice are cast. The number 12 means much to a baker, to a foot rule, or in a court case. Sweet 16 is an appealing number . . . and so on: 23, 36, 45, 50-50, 52 and other numbers ad infinitum.

In North Carolina and to North Carolinians the world over, a never-to-be-forgotten number is 22.

Folks who don't know the number of Apostles or the number of Books in the Bible can tell you about 22. As long as there is a Chapel

Hill the number 22 will mean "Charlie Justice"—"the Will-'o-the-Wisp of Kenan Stadium"—the most thrilling athlete in the history of the University of North Carolina.

Once an octogenarian in the western part of the State was asked how he'd like to celebrate his ninetieth birthday and he replied: "I'd like to go to Chapel Hill and get one good look at Number 22 before I die . . ."

Maybe, Charlie Justice's great appeal is the David and Goliath bit all over again—the little guy who slew giants . . . Whatever it is let this book tell the Justice Story. And what a story!

Wherever sports are played, and as long as sports are played, men will tell the Justice Story over and over and over and over . . .

And forever Chapel Hillians will sing the swing-coda of Alma Mater:

> "He's a Tar Heel born
> And a Tar Heel bred
> And when he dies
> He'll be a Tar Heel—immortal."

W. D. CARMICHAEL, JR.

INTRODUCTION

On the face of it, Charlie (Choo Choo) Justice belongs to another era. Although the seasons 1946 through 1949 appear to be but a short punt into the past, the years since have given rise to new gridiron heroes and to a whole new generation of football lovers. During the Justice heyday, Choo Choo Justice T-shirts thrilled the small fry—but today those youngsters who proudly flaunted Choo Choo on their chests are themselves members of high school football teams, reaching for their own fame. Perhaps one or two of them are playing on this year's University of North Carolina freshman squad. To them the remarkable feats of Justice the player are as remote as the powerful slugging of Joe DiMaggio, the Yankee Clipper, or the velvet-smooth trombone notes of the great T. Dorsey.

But altogether time has been good to the Justice story. Thousands upon thousands of University students, old grads, and just plain fans took the great Choo Choo into their hearts, and they have never forgotten him. Fondly they recall those crisp and boisterous autumn afternoons when this brilliant, graceful sportsman tore cheers of delight from their carefree throats.

Not only are his feats remembered today, but Justice himself is still an extremely popular individual. He can walk down the main street of almost any North Carolina hamlet and someone will walk up and say, "Hi, Choo Choo, what are you doing in town?"

Coutless thousands—perhaps millions—of words have been written about the Asheville boy, and the authors of this book have long talked of putting the story together in one volume.

There are few sportswriters in the area who have not thought of this at one time or another and projects similar to this were dreamed of and planned while Justice's name still roamed the headlines of the daily press.

Some will wonder why this book has been written at this late date. It has been written in an effort to record the story before already-faded newspaper clippings and fading memories blot out the real truth and fancy takes hold of the mind.

It has been written because the authors feel there are many who would like to re-read the story and pass it along to their sports-loving youngsters.

It has been written because the authors have a notion that Justice is already a part of North Carolina folklore—and contemporary history and folklore should be carefully chronicled.

In his own medium, Justice is as much a part of North Carolina as Tom Wolfe and Charles Aycock and Kay Kyser.

The authors have attempted to rekindle the mood and spirit of the Justice era—the time on the University of North Carolina campus when the heart of even the more mature student was young and gay and full to the brim with the joy of being home from "the War" and at Chapel Hill.

Our bibliography is our memories, our talks with the subject, and dusty newspaper files in the dark, damp basement of *The Charlotte News* and the contrastingly bright stacks of the fine Charlotte Public Library.

Our acknowledgements are many, but most pointedly to two groups. First, we acknowledge the work of the sportswriters and sportscasters of the state and country who told the story at the time. Their words afforded research material—plus many hours of reading pleasure.

Next we acknowledge the role played by more than one hundred football players—and especially the very unsung substitutes at tailback—of the Justice era. We regret that all of them could not be mentioned in the text, for they deserve to be singled out individually.

Finally, there are five individuals to whom we express our most sincere thanks.

Orville Campbell, Chapel Hill publisher and jack-of-all trades, has made valuable contributions to the book. His keen insight—he was Charlie's closest campus friend—and interest were most helpful.

Photographer Hugh Morton, certainly one of the best in the United States, took memorable Justice photographs. We thank him for the use of many in this volume and for his judgment in the over-all selection of photographic art.

Jake Wade wrote more about and for Charlie than anyone else. He wrote, in those excitingly hectic days, not publicity releases, but prose poems to the athlete. His advice and counsel were appreciated.

Dr. Sam Barnes, wrestling coach and English professor, and George F. Scheer, author and historian, assisted in the development of the manuscript with good enthusiasm and criticism.

JULIAN SCHEER
BOB QUINCY

Charlotte, N. C.
September 5, 1958

CHOO CHOO
The Charlie Justice Story

I

A VALENTINE FOR 'KING CARL'

It began one chilly afternoon in Kenan Stadium and the clock of the Bell Tower, peering over the foliage like a straight-backed, sedate judge, set the time at 4 p.m. Leaves had turned for it was February, 1946, and winter had come to Chapel Hill.

A young man was on trial.

The courtroom was a football field and the defendant chose to represent himself.

That was the beginning of Justice for North Carolina.

AS A PHYSICAL specimen, Charlie Justice was far less impressive than the average of 150 or more padded, helmeted football players assembled at mid-field for a scrimmage between Guilford College, the small Quaker school near Greensboro, and the University of North Carolina. The Tar Heels were winding up winter drills.

Carl Snavely, colorfully tagged "the Gray Fox" and "King Carl," was in his second year of coaching the Carolinians since his recall from Cornell. The taciturn Snavely passed a few friendly words with Doc Newton, his counterpart at Guilford, then blew a whistle as a signal to open the attack.

Newcomer Justice was not listed among the early combatants. He stood near the sidelines, his hands shoved deep into the pockets of his parka for warmth. The Quakers opened the offense, and Justice watched with a detachment characteristic of a person not too familiar with his surroundings.

"There he is over there, the little guy," said a student to his friends huddled in the lower stands. The seats were cold and some spectators were standing, shoulder to shoulder. There may have been 1,000 at the trial. Most had come to witness Charlie Justice handle pigskin.

"He's not even first string," said a bystander. "If he's the hottest football property in America, why isn't he a starter?"

In the early minutes, Guilford moved the ball well. Snavely, an expression of scorn on his face, seemed disturbed. The session meant nothing in wins and losses, but a successful workout would be a deciding factor in morale, both for the squad and the campus.

Snavely had a mission. He hadn't been lured from Cornell to build character. North Carolina alumni and students and backers were hungry for victory.

"Justice," snapped Snavely when the ball was taken by the Tar Heels on their own 35. The 165-pounder walked toward the coach head down, an ear cocked to one side like a fox terrier awaiting instructions from its master.

"Try tailback for a while," directed the coach.

It was a routine substitution, but a hush fell over the stands.

Guilford dug in, determined to stop the most sought-after prospect in Southern football history. It was a moment when a fumble would seem to be inevitable.

The ball was snapped to Justice, as everyone had suspected.

He moved to his right, gathered speed for four steps, and suddenly peeled from formation like a dive-bomber sighting a target. The gap between tackle and end was open. It closed, but not on Justice. He quickly moved into the secondary and was on his own.

A linebacker lunged at a hip, which pulled away like a shy girl. A halfback raced across the field, lowered his head, and made a solo landing, his arms clasping air.

Five, ten yards downfield, Justice sized up the Quaker safety man. He ran directly at him, applying a head and shoulder fake as he breezed within reach. The confused defender took it as if cued by a hypnotist. Past the last line of resistance, Choo Choo angled for the sidelines all alone.

When Justice stepped into the end zone, his dash was measured at 65 yards. There was a stunned silence in the stands as the onlookers tried to reconstruct the almost effortless trial run. Then a spontaneous cheer arose. It became the first in four years of loud, exuberant noise dedicated to a halfback wearing No. 22.

A few took time to notice Snavely. The Dutchman, normally reserved and poised, was leaping about in jubilation. He met Justice at the sidelines, threw his arm around the shoulders of the halfback and cried, "That's enough, that's enough! Good boy, good boy!"

2

The band sounded off—as Charlie came marching on

Justice had humbled his critics with one dynamic piece of evidence, the first and only required for acquittal.

North Carolina thus set sail on her finest voyage in football.

*   *   *

The Justice era, sometimes referred to as the Golden days of North Carolina football, started in 1946 and lasted through 1949. During that time the Tar Heels won 32 games, lost seven, and tied two. They attended three Bowls and could have gone to a fourth.

Talent was immense, and Snavely, who was one of the remaining disciplinarians of the single wing attack, had in the Choo Choo the perfect engineer to run his rugged railroad.

For four seasons Justice upheld the most flattering and demanding press of any player in Southern football history.

He scored 234 points during his career, 72 of them as a freshman.

He passed or ran for 65 touchdowns, 26 of them sailing through the air, with Art Weiner, a lanky, wise-cracking flankman from Newark, N. J., his principal target.

As a ball carrier, Charlie sidetepped foes for 2,814 yards during his four years or the equivalent of 1.6 miles.

He compiled a total offense record of 5,176 yards, and, just to keep the defense loose, punted on 251 occasions for a four-year average of 42.5 per kick.

There have been better runners, better passers and better kickers in the history of football, but Charlie Justice had few peers as a triple-threat operative. He was just another citizen as he walked the streets or sat at home in an easy chair. But once he held a football, something wonderful happened.

Perhaps it was the time in history for a player of Justice's stature to capture the appeal of the masses. World War II had come to an end. The hysteria for uniforms and medals and stories of dogfights with the Zero had worn a trifle thin. The boom years were on in sports. Professional baseball was a thriving business. Colleges began thinking in terms of Coliseum-type structures for their invigorated basketball programs in a game that had zoomed to new popularity.

It wasn't a time for Frank Merriwell, the bright-eyed schoolboy. He had had his day. The more mature, believable champion was in vogue.

Charlie Justice was cut of a pattern the nation could take to its bosom.

He was a veteran who had been overseas.

He was married and settled, but boyish and still pursuing an education.

He was modest. He was a "Lil David" who could befuddle giants.

He had good looks, a chin chiseled to perfection for photographers and artists.

He dressed well. He was friendly.

And what's more, he was as home grown as tobacco from Rocky Mount, towels from Kannapolis, furniture from High Point, and moonshine from Wilkes County.

Charlie Justice was more than an ordinary football player when he entered the University in the winter of 1946. At Lee Edwards High in Asheville, he led the Maroons to two unbeaten seasons, was named to All-Southern prep teams both years, and at the age of 17 had college scouts standing in line for autographs.

He would have attended college had there not been a war and other obligations. The Navy rated his services, and he was shipped to Bainbridge Naval Training Center in Maryland. There he had to insist on a tryout for the football squad. Once his talents were noticed, he became the baby-faced star of a pro-studded team.

After three years of sensational notices in service football, Justice could name his next stop. The Washington Redskins and Philadelphia Eagles tempted him with professional offers. Scouts from colleges too numerous to list deluged him with flattering proposals.

Why did he choose North Carolina?

"In my lifetime I made two wise choices," said Justice. "One was marrying my wife, Sarah. The other was to attend North Carolina. Sarah was my idea and mine alone. I needed advice from my brother Jack on picking the right school."

The scramble began when Charlie returned from Hawaii in December of 1945. He called Sarah, his spouse of two years, from San Francisco and happily broke the news he would soon be with her in Asheville.

"I'm taking the train, honey," he said, "and seeing you and the family means everything to me. Please, please don't tell anyone I'm coming. I want this vacation to be ours. It's real flattering, but these college scouts are on me everywhere I turn. If I go into a restaurant to eat, they're ready to take my order before the waiter is. When I get home, let's go away for a week and forget football."

The ride was long and tedious. Seats were scarce and the holiday traffic during the war years tested the patience of the railroad and its passengers.

Finally, Asheville.

Seaman Justice pushed his sea bag down the aisle and his heart beat faster with each step. Rest, relaxation, the calm of being with one's family stirred his emotions.

He reached the exit of the Pullman and lowered his gear. Where was Sarah?

"Hi, Charlie," said a fellow with a wide smile, thick shoulders and thinning red hair.

"Dan Hill . . . Dan Hill . . . what the blazes are you doing here?" gasped Justice as he looked at the assistant athletic director from Duke.

"Why, you know what I'm here for," said Dan. "We want you to attend Duke, Charlie. We'd like you to play a little football for us, too."

Justice was amazed at the recruiting tenacity and resourcefulness of Hill, an Asheville product himself, who had made All-American at the Durham institution as a center. Only Sarah had known the whereabouts of her husband. She had told no one.

"Dan," said Charlie, "you're working for the wrong folks."

"What do you mean?" grinned Hill.

"You should be with the FBI. A spy wouldn't have a chance."

Justice begged off a commitment to Hill, finally located Sarah and his family. As he was driving home he began thinking of Dan's impromptu welcome. He realized he wouldn't have a spare moment until he made a choice of schools.

The next month was frantic. Justice answered the telephone almost constantly to greet coaches, politely refuse propositions, or accept invitations to visit various campuses.

When the weeding procedure came to an end, three schools remained as possibilities. They were North Carolina, South Carolina, and Duke.

Jack Justice, the oldest brother, was the deciding force in the ultimate decision.

"Jack was more than just a brother," explained Charlie. "He was more of a father during my younger days. My original thinking favored South Carolina. I had returned from a visit to Columbia and I was impressed. So was Sarah. Rex Enright was a charming host."

Jack found Charlie in the kitchen, making a sandwich.

"You've decided?" he asked.

"I think so."

"Let me say one thing," said Jack, quite seriously. "I've tried all my life to guide you along the right track. I went to Rollins and I liked it there. But I'm a North Carolina citizen and I'll always regret not attending a school in this state.

"If you plan to return to Asheville to live, Charlie, you choose a college in this state. That's my final piece of advice. Make up your own mind, but, if you go elsewhere, just forget I'm in the family. Don't ever come to me again with your problems."

The brief lecture jolted Charlie. He talked with Sarah and they agreed, since the matter had taken on a seriousness within the family itself, it would be either Duke or North Carolina.

"One more thing," said Jack one evening. "I don't think you'd enjoy playing football for Wallace Wade. He's a great coach, but, for a fellow of your size, I think you'd stand a better chance of succeeding under Snavely. He won't demand so much power in football."

Charlie wasn't convinced.

North Carolina, during the wooing period, had seemed indifferent in comparison with other schools. Coach Snavely, who often gave first-acquaintances the impression of being cool and preoccupied, had been polite, but had made no overtures.

"I'm not sure they want me at Carolina, Jack," Charlie said. He cited a meeting with Assistant Athletic Director Chuck Erickson and the coach. They were to drive him to the airport for a return to Asheville.

7

ach Snavely, Trainer Quinlan and their favorite horse

"When we got in the automobile," said Charlie, "Mr. Erickson asked me to sit up front with Coach Snavely. He sat in the back with Sarah. We got started on the drive which lasted about twenty minutes."

Erickson and Sarah chatted pleasantly.

Said Snavely, turning his head toward Justice: "How much do you weigh, Charlie?"

"About 165, sir," said Justice.

Snavely pursed his lips. He drove and drove . . . but there was no more conversation.

Jack Justice laughed. Said he: "Snavely was just thinking, Charlie. He likes you, I know that."

Charlie took his time and finally reached a decision.

"I'll go to North Carolina," he informed Jack one evening.

When the announcement was made Jake Wade of *The Charlotte Observer* wrote: "Carl Snavely got the nicest Valentine of any coach in the country."

The date was February 14.

The news of Charlie Justice's selection of a school made headlines across the nation.

Some columnists said he had been bought with a good portion of the gold in Fort Knox.

Others cried bitterly he had sold to the highest bidder and had broken promises.

The happy ones predicted All-American honors his first year.

Conservatives and the disgruntled foresaw the 165-pound package being crumpled in his first varsity shipment.

"He'll never make the grade," a prominent coach was quoted as saying. "Players will resent him and won't block for him. He's too accustomed to the pro style he learned at Bainbridge to accept the college brand of football."

It was under such conditions that Charlie arrived at Chapel Hill. He knew few people on the campus, yet everyone knew him.

The circumstances would have disturbed a youngster of less ambition.

Snavely underplayed his own part in the drama to the point of it becoming a national joke. A reporter confronted the coach at his office in Woollen Gymnasium and asked him what he thought of Justice entering Carolina.

"I understand more than 50 name colleges were after him, Coach," said the newsman, his pencil and pad ready for action. "What do you have to say about his coming here?"

Snavely cleared his throat, looked at the ceiling, and set his blue eyes into a motionless stare.

"I hope," said King Carl, "he decides to come out for football."

8

Several days later some fun-poking students at Duke, let down by Justice's ultimate choice but still owning a tart sense of humor, wrote an open letter to the editor of the student paper.

"We would like to urge Mr. Justice," they said, "to try the game of football—along with his studies. He may find he will take to it and, who knows, he may even make the team!"

Carl Snavely was haunted by his quote for the next four seasons.

The way things turned out, he didn't mind at all.

II

THE JUSTICE ERA BEGINS

Charlie Justice didn't build Kenan in the manner that Babe Ruth "constructed" Yankee Stadium in New York, but no individual in the picturesque arena's lifetime can be more closely associated with its success.

The Justice appearance became a symbol of box office might. Other than Notre Dame, North Carolina claimed more "subway" alumni than any school in the country from 1946 through 1949.

They came to see Charlie run, pass and kick. There was seldom a dull moment.

* * *

KENAN TURF had always been kind to Charlie. There was that opening run against Guilford in his first practice game—his one and only play during the winter workout.

In the spring, a Blue and White skirmish was held. More than 3,000, an unheard of number for an intra-squad battle, came to scrutinize Snavely's finest in action. Once again, Justice stirred the imagination.

On his first play from scrimmage, he went the distance, 64 yards in all. The Justice-led Whites trampled the Blues 33-0.

Few fans realized that Charlie had been introduced to the pine-secluded hollow two years before he chose the University for his undergraduate capers. He was a member of Bainbridge's vaunted Navy team at the time. The game was held in the fall of 1944 against North Carolina Pre-Flight.

The fullback and leader for the Pre-Flight team was to become a close personal friend of Justice's, a fellow named Otto Graham, later one of the all-time greats of professional football. Graham and Company were highly ranked. They had as many stars as Bainbridge.

Justice, a gob with fuzz on his face, didn't start against Otto and his pro-polished teammates. He fidgeted on the bench, tense as usual, and watched the opening ceremonies.

When Coach Joe Maniaci decided to utilize the scatback, the audience, basically cadets, since travel limitations prevented sizeable civilian gatherings, began buzzing. Even in pads, this young man looked undernourished, unfit for land or sea duty.

Charlie played less than nine minutes. He scored one touchdown on a run of 38 yards, probed the Pre-Flight secondary for several sizeable gains, and was a leader in a staggering 49-20 victory.

"Get lost, kid," ordered Maniaci, when he took out Choo Choo. "Get lost before some admiral sees you and tries to get you transferred."

Charlie didn't realize it, but he was getting his cleats into soil that would be the stage for four years of college sorcery and daring.

When football practice began in late August of 1946, there were writers picking North Carolina to go all the way, chiefly on the basis of Justice's arrival.

"My goodness," Snavely sighed. "Give the boy a chance. We know he can run—but this is a sport which requires 11 men doing a job. We won five games last year and didn't have half the schedule. We have a building job ahead."

The pressure, nonetheless, was on the coach.

And it was on Charlie Justice.

Justice was no prima donna, although many who envied him would occasionally term him one. He had received good schooling from his brother Jack on that count and never had to be told a halfback's best friend is the blocker in front of him.

Before the opening game of his freshman season against Virginia Tech, Charlie knew his comrades-in-arms well. He had made sure of his personal touch when he joined the squad the previous February.

"I didn't ask for the buildup I got on entering Carolina," he said, "but it was there and I could do nothing about it. There was some resentment. I know human nature that well. I felt the best thing I could do was to meet the players quickly and get to know them."

Charlie began learning names, hometowns, faces. Two days after his first introduction to the squad, he could call most of the players by their first names. He spoke before being spoken to. He shouted encouragement and compliments on the field.

12

Charlie and his rugged backfield mate, Walt Pu[

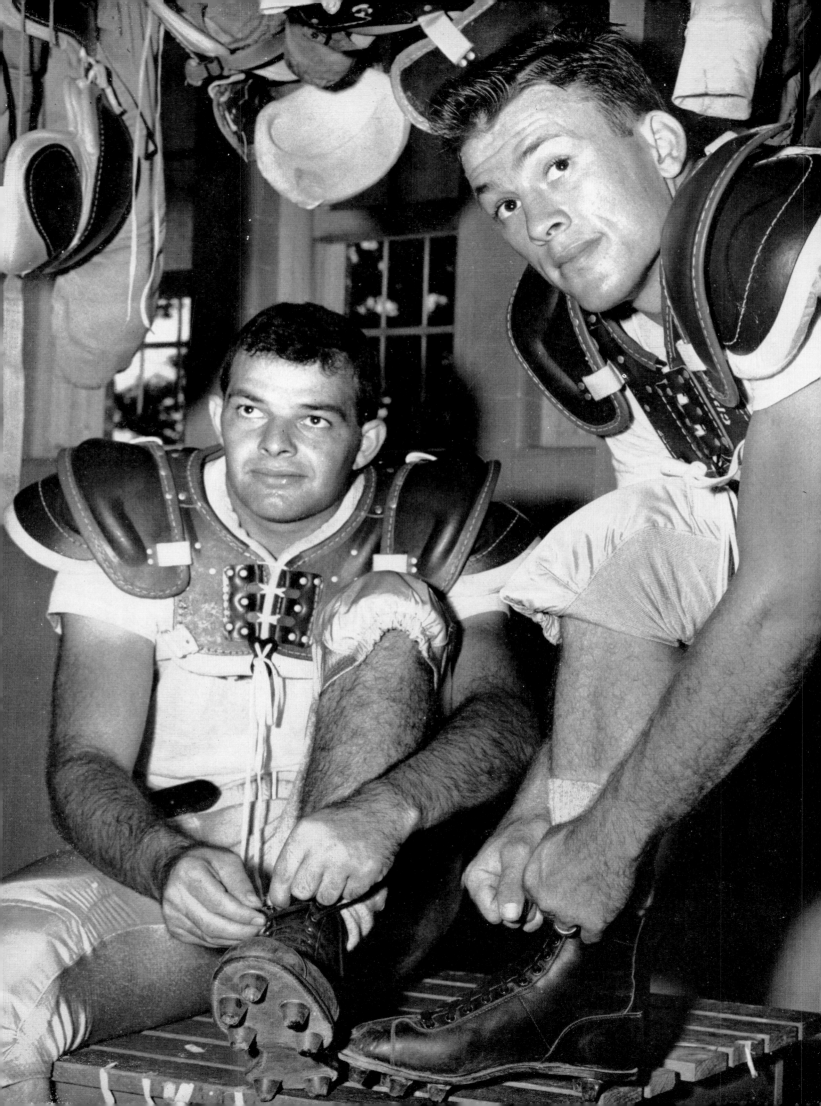

He was a natural sparkplug.

What's more, he loved the game, despite the beatings he took and the bumps that came far more often than the headlines. A football was the only toy Charlie knew and the gridiron was his playground.

Morris Mason, who was beginning his 18th season in the equipment room when Choo Choo was handed his famed No. 22 jersey, was quick to note the ambition and desire of Justice.

"He was always the first one to dress," said Mason, "and the last one to come off the practice field. He was something, that Mista Justice. He could do about everything and he never quit trying to improve.

"I been here a long time. There was Johnny Branch. Now Mista Branch could run about as fast as anybody ever, especially when he got back there and caught a punt. But everytime Mista Branch got the ball, you knew what was gonna happen.

"Now Mista Justice was different. He might get it and run, or get it and kick, or get it and pass. Nobody knew what Mista Justice was gonna do but Mista Justice. And he never told nobody."

Chapel Hill was a lively but somewhat abnormal college community when matriculation began in 1946.

Veterans were returning in numbers, many of them still wearing their "ruptured ducks." There were more married students than ever before. This, with a normal complement of the high school youth parade, presented a conflict in personalities on the campus.

The common denominator was the football team. Success on the playing field would unite the odd-balls of the campus, the playboys, the cynical veterans, and the honest-to-goodness students.

This was the job ahead for Charlie Justice and his teammates. Perhaps the most overlooked segment of Charlie's career is that he helped create a campus spirit that has never been equalled. Never before had so many students had so little in common— and got along so smoothly together.

The Virginia Tech opener was a case of untimely scheduling. The Gobblers, too, had hopes of becoming a grid power, but few took them seriously. The Tar Heels weren't up to the occasion, and what many termed a breather became a nightmare.

Justice flashed brilliance, dashed for a 68-yard touchdown and set up another. But he had two kicks blocked by a burly tackle named John Maskas, who was a destroyer all afternoon, and both were converted into VPI touchdowns.

The final score was a deadlock, 14-14.

Was Justice a failure? Had the myth fizzled? With such foes as Miami, Navy, Tennessee, and Duke ahead, the Tar Heels would improve or else!

During the coaches' meeting the next day, one of the assistants let off steam.

"We've made a mistake on Justice," he ranted. "He doesn't have it. He's a hot shot who knows only one thing—to grab the ball and run. He'll never fit our system and we ought to get rid of him now, before we get in too deep."

14

Snavely stroked his chin.

"I don't agree," injected Max Reed, a little guy with gray hair who had been with Snavely at Cornell. "That was one game. We weren't prepared. What more could be expected of a ball player? Did Justice block those kicks himself?"

The argument continued until Snavely called a halt.

"Let's get ready for Miami," he ordered, "and I do mean get ready. We know our shortcomings. One of them isn't the tailback. Charlie Justice is our tailback until someone beats him out—and I personally don't think there's anyone around who can do it."

The Tar Heels traveled into Florida's depths for the Miami contest at the Orange Bowl. The game offered much speculation. It was to become the launching platform for the Justice era of razzle-dazzle.

Virginia Tech had made the most of poor Tar Heel kicking technique. Miami would do likewise, Carolina coaches felt, unless, unless . . .

"Charlie," reasoned Coach Reed just before the kickoff, "this Miami club has those blocked punts on its mind. It's logical. Now if we don't get anywhere the first two downs, drop back in kick formation. You have an option of booting or running. See what happens."

Miami elected to kick and Justice took it at the goal, returning to the 34. Two plays into the middle failed. Third and nine. The tailback dropped back.

Charlie took the center snap from Chan Highsmith, the captain for the evening, and faked a step as if to boot. The Miami ends crashed. The outside was as clear as a desert highway.

Justice needed no prompting. With his blocking making the road easy, it was a 65-yard sprint for a touchdown that stunned the Hurricane. There was no recovery. The game wound up 21-0, and Justice, featuring dashes of 27 and 29 yards, gained a grand total of 206 yards.

Wrote Luther Evans in the *Miami Herald* the next morning: "North Carolina showed Miami plenty of Justice but little mercy."

Said Coach Snavely: "I feel a lot better than I did last week."

A weak Maryland team visited Chapel Hill the next week and skies were dark. Rain poured throughout the game and Snavely kept his prize left half under wraps as if fearing his uniform would shrink. It was a good move for all concerned. The score was 33-0 in favor of the Tar Heels and the press was allowed the sage comment: "CAROLINA NO ONE-MAN TEAM."

Maryland's only threat was a passing whiz named Tommy Mont, who completed 18 of 36 tosses under the worst conditions. Mont was destined to become head coach at the College Park institution.

It was icy in Baltimore's Municipal Stadium on October 18. Cold everywhere except on the field, where the Tar Heels needed 14 points in a hot fourth quarter to overcome a Navy lead and win by 21-14.

Justice scored the first touchdown with a short run. The last two were furnished by the slashing, driving legs of Fullback Walt Pupa, who did most of the carrying while Choo Choo faked the Navy defense.

It was as rough as a battle between two wild boars. Dick Scott, Navy's All-American center, took particular delight in slamming Justice about. The Tar Heels returned to Chapel Hill happy—but bruised.

"It was the making of our team," said Charlie. "For the first time, I really felt we had that extra something called greatness. Everyone realized I wasn't the entire show, that Walt and the line and real guts made us click. We barely got by Navy, but we had become a team."

Ray (Bear) Wolf brought his Florida 'Gators to Chapel Hill the next week, and the story pictured the former North Carolina coach determined to "upset" the school which had bid him goodbye after he entered service in 1941. He was 21 points wrong. Carolina won by a landslide, 40-19.

Justice had a dash of 75 yards from scrimmage for a touchdown and a second-half kickoff return of 90 for a score. Commented Wolf to the *AP's* Whitney Martin, who wrote a Monday column called "The Old Professor": "It was simply a case of too much Justice."

It became a standard phrase for many coaches.

North Carolina lost its first game the next week, 20-14, to Tennessee. The night before the contest, Justice paced the Pullman car which carried the Tar Heels over the mountains into Knoxville. He was suffering from an upset stomach and the late Dick (Doc) White served as nursemaid.

Still, that afternoon at Shields-Watkins Field brings memories to those who saw Charlie make what many consider his most dazzling and awesome gallop, the 74-yard sprint which found him weaving back and forth across the field like an educated mouse in a maze. No less than 13 Volunteers had their hands on him and failed to hold on.

"Shucks," said Justice in the dressing room, emotionally let down after the loss. "Anyone can make a run if the blocking's there."

General Bob Neyland, the great Tennessee coach, compared it with the all-time spectacular run the Vols' Johnny Butler made against Alabama in pre-war years. Butler reversed his field three times in going some 56 yards to score.

Charlie, however, can't forget his own defensive flaw that cost the Tar Heels the deciding touchdown. Safety Walter Salter took one of his punts late in the game and seemingly stepped out of bounds. The defense sagged—and Slater continued on his way, still very much in operation. Justice was the last defensive man between Walt, later a coach at North Carolina State, and pay stripes. Behind Slater was another Vol, End Jim Powell.

As Justice braced to make the tackle, the Tennessee man yelled, "Lateral it." Slater faked a pitch—and Charlie took the fake. Walter scored standing, a 78-yard run.

17

wo punts blocked in game number one, but none ever again

As he reached the end zone, Slater turned and grinned at Justice. An alert photographer caught the action as Charlie made a futile effort for the runner wearing the big smile.

It became one of the most publicized pictures of the season. Justice, a victim of a two-on-one situation, had to bite his pride and become the "goat" of a compromising defensive position.

Carolina, with an abundance of material, pulled a "surprise" the next week against William and Mary and didn't start Justice, rather opened with Billy Britt, a fellow Ashevillian, at left half. Later Charlie came in, "fed" the ball to Wingback Jim Camp on a series of reverse patterns, and baffled the Indians with new tactics.

The Tar Heels led by three touchdowns at one stage, wound up in front by 21-7.

Wake Forest, coached by D. C. (Peahead) Walker and playing a thunderous, bone-shattering type game, allowed Red Cochran to match punts and runs with Justice the next Saturday. Playing before a shouting mob in perfect weather, the game rated as the finest spectacle of the year.

North Carolina won, 26-14, but the 60 minutes of football offered everything. Coach Walker, garbed in a loud shirt and a tie that made a rainbow seem modest and pale, smoked enough cigarettes to overload an ash tray the size of a pumpkin.

In the first period against the Deacs, Justice got off punts of 65 and 58 yards. He set up a first-quarter touchdown with a 62-yard run, the result of a fake boot. He scored minutes later on a pass from Pupa.

On the last play of the game, he took the ball on the Wake 20, danced, side-stepped and weaved through most of the Deacons for a touchdown.

Not since 1940, when Joe Austin caught a Jim Lalanne pass to upset the Blue Devils, 6-3, had North Carolina beaten Duke. What would the superman called Justice do when the chips were really on the table?

He played a gambling hand. He was constantly on the go, kicking, passing, electrifying the crowd with his move to break open the contest. It was as rough as expected. A Justice pass to slim John Tandy, the end, made it an even first half, 7-7.

Carolina broke loose for 15 points in the fourth frame to wrap it up. One touchdown was the result of a Justice handoff to right half Jack Fitch on a reverse. Another came on a 17-yard run, with Choo Choo sidestepping Duke tacklers like a pickpocket in a subway. A safety was the concluder, and North Carolina had its first victory in six years, 22-7.

Happy days were in Chapel Hill again!

Virginia was easy prey the final game, but Justice came off the trainer's table to conduct one of his finest tours.

An *Associated Press* dispatch from Chapel Hill in mid-week informed the public that "Justice is not expected to punt or run against Virginia because he is nursing a wrenched knee from the Duke game."

Blocking back Joe Wright leads Justice on a run against Tennessee

"Injured" Charlie had dashes of 56, 40 and 18 yards against the Cavaliers and a total of 170 yards in 17 carries.

Huffed a tired Virginian at the conclusion: "If Justice can run like that with a wrenched knee, there's no telling how good he could be with a pair wrenched."

That afternoon the All-Southern team was announced and Justice was a unanimous choice. Others in the backfield were Nick Sacrinty of Wake Forest, Howard Turner of North Carolina State, and Jack Cloud of William and Mary.

The victory over Virginia set the Tar Heels in a landlordish position for bowl bids. They had choices of several and agreed the Sugar would be sweetest.

It resulted in one of the most bitter and controversial losses of the Justice era.

III

A BOWL OF BITTER SUGAR

History tells of great Carolina teams in the past, All-Americans like George Barclay, Paul Severin, Andy Bershak.

But this was the first bowl bid.

It was a dream come true for Tar Heel fans and for stoic Carl Snavely who had barely missed the pot of gold in the past.

It was, also, a big moment for a weak-tootin' trombone player in the University band. Director Earl Slocum took him on the trip, even though his musicianship left much to be desired.

Andy Griffith strutted like a Teagarden that day in New Orleans, later wrote a best-selling ditty called "What It Was, Was Football" and rode to fame on Broadway and in Hollywood.

*   *   *   *   *   *

NEW ORLEANS is a gay, quaint, unsophisticated city which has welcomed pirates with the same friendliness that it has offered diplomats since the time of the Buccaneers.

It had never been confronted, however, with such rowdy partisans as the visiting forces from Georgia and North Carolina those few days before the Sugar Bowl game of 1947.

Hardened policemen winced, little old ladies ran for cover and night clubs enjoyed the brisk business of Mardi Gras. A number of Tar Heels became students of architecture during this sojourn, chiefly that of the Cat Girl, a lady of unusual structure who was on exhibit each night in the French quarter.

Some of the most heated debates in the South since Clarence Darrow engaged William Jennings Bryan transpired. Subject: the greatest Charlie—Trippi of Georgia or Justice of North Carolina.

Sizable amounts of money changed hands on the betting market. Georgia, with a 15-game winning streak, rated a slight edge in bookmaking. At game time, five and six points were given the Tar Heels.

While the students were having the time of their lives—and a staggering number of them managed transportation from Chapel Hill to the Louisiana port—the football squad encamped at Gulfport, Mississippi, some 60 miles to the east. Never had they been worked so hard and heard of so much fun.

Coach Snavely was all business. There are critics who contend the Tar Heels reached the fine edge of perfection several days before game time, then lost it to practice fatigue.

The Tar Heels were deep in manpower, although two of their regulars were absent. Art Weiner, the sure-fingered flankman, quit the squad at the end of the regular season because of personal problems and dropped from school temporarily. He was missed, but no position on the Carolina roster was better protected than end. Chan Highsmith, the center, was out with a spinal injury and was in a back cast.

The first day of January, 1947, was murky and damp. There were times when actual play was hard to distinguish from the stands, especially for those among the 73,000 who were assigned to seats in the clouds of the stadium.

The game, won by Georgia after the Bulldogs twice came from behind, kept the crowd in a frenzy for 60 minutes. Not until the dying seconds did it seem that all was lost for the Tar Heels.

When Trippi made his first appearance on the turf, the Georgia stands gave a 21-gun salute. Carolina managed 22 for its hero, Choo Choo.

UNC went to work with upset in mind, hoping to make Trippi the goat. In the second quarter, Guard Bob Mitten of the Tar Heels corralled a Trippi jump pass on the Georgia 25. The break was quickly converted into a score as Walt Pupa slashed his way over left guard for the first score. A Bob Cox conversion made it 7-0 and that's the way it read at halftime.

A play which pulled the Bulldogs from behind in the third period became the most controversial one in the four-year Justice era. It upset the North Carolina team tremendously when the decision now known as the "forward-lateral incident," went in favor of Georgia.

"Georgia beat us by 10 points," shrugged a member of Snavely's coaching staff at the conclusion, "and that is a clear cut advantage. Yet, we weren't the same team after that disputed play. Georgia knew it and drove it down our throats. The emotional side of football wins as often as the physical side."

22

Joe Tereshinski, Georgia's right end who was a menace as a defensive player all afternoon, intercepted a Pupa pass on his own 24. Seeing he was caught, he looked for lateral possibilities and found Fullback Dick McPhee moving up fast. He flipped the ball in desperation.

McPhee seemed to have the way cleared for him, but somehow Dan Steigman, the UNC center, got to him on the 14. Two plays later Johnny Rauch sneaked over from the quarterback post with the evening marker.

Carolina players howled that McPhee was in front of Tereshinski when he took the pitch—and that it constituted a forward maneuver rather than the legal lateral. A game official had pulled his handkerchief, started to throw it to earth, then changed his mind, they pointed out.

The stands were making so much noise by this time it was hard to discuss the topic on the field. Coach Snavely, his face the color of a freshly painted fireplug, was incensed. Players milled about and looked toward the bench. Some kicked dirt, others threw their helmets to their feet in disgust.

The Georgia advancement was within legal limits, ruled the policemen in stripes, and it would hold.

Later, both sides developed game film and offered "positive proof" that: (1) the lateral was most certainly a lateral in every respect, and (2) that the "lateral" was most certainly a forward pass in every respect. It depended upon which camp one followed.

Georgians like to point out that if the incident upset the Tar Heels so much, they surely didn't act like it in the next series of plays. After the kickoff, Carolina took the ball, with Justice, Jim Camp at wing and Fullback Pupa alternating, to move to the opposition's 14. There the Bulldogs became tough, indeed.

End Bob Cox, later to become national president of the Junior Chamber of Commerce (1958), kicked an 18-yard field goal and North Carolina led, 10-7.

The young men coached by Wally Butts had found life in that third period score and were ready to pull all stops. Three minutes later, Trippi fired a bullet pass to End Dan Edwards. He picked up fine blocking at the Carolina 44 and went all the way, untouched.

In the fourth quarter, with Tar Heel players still living in the past and challenging the officials as to the forward-lateral, Georgia got an insurance score. It would have come earlier had not Justice hauled down Trippi, who had broken away, on the Georgia 42.

Wrote George Barton of the *Minneapolis Tribune*: "Charley Trippi triumphed over Charlie Justice in their duel for individual honors. Georgia's great All-American halfback lugged the ball 77 yards in 15 attempts against 37 yards in 18 tries for Justice.

"However, sturdy little Justice proved to all and sundry he is everything written about him during the season. He is fast as a streak and elusive as a jackrabbit—a touchdown threat every time he takes the ball. The Bulldogs, coached by Butts to keep Justice under control, did a nifty job of it, but they had to be on the alert every second."

Chief flagman for the Choo Choo that day was the crashing Tereshinski, a flankman who liked it rough. Some years later, when they were teammates as Washington Redskins, Justice commented to Joe he saw more than enough of him during the Sugar Bowl.

"That figures," said Tereshinski.

"What do you mean?" said Justice.

"Simply that I had a job," answered Joe. "My assignment on every play was to get to you and tackle you whether you had the ball or not."

"You did a great job," grunted Justice. "I spent more time with you in New Orleans than I did my wife."

While neither Justice nor Trippi scored a point in the game, both offered evidence of greatness in all fields of play. Trippi, labeled the "Scintillating Sicilian," played the full 60 minutes. Justice was in action 53 minutes.

The Sugar Bowl committee, in listing its All-Time All-Stars, placed Justice and Trippi on the first team for the group covering the years 1945-1954. Leon Heath of Oklahoma and Harry Gilmer of Alabama are backs completing the foursome.

Losing the Sugar Bowl game provided the first season of Justice with an anticlimactic finish, but in retrospect the over-all job done by Snavely and his staff was the most significant one in the history of the University.

Thanks to the Bowl payday, more money had been made than at any other time in UNC football history. The athletic department was in excellent shape—and during the next three years the "black" side of the budget was to show a $500,000 profit, thanks chiefly to the Justice lure.

What was even more pleasing to Snavely was that Justice, with all his publicity clips, had been a model football player. His conduct off the playing field was all any coach could hope for in a star.

The little tailback from Asheville neither smoked nor drank. He was a popular figure in the village and on the campus. He spoke frankly but with a certain modesty that won him friends. He never discussed a touchdown run without recalling the individual who made the key block.

Asked by a prominent newspaperman to write a guest column one day, Charlie began: "I feel out of place doing this—just as much as I would be in carrying the ball without good guards and tackles paving the way."

The first year of Justice at Chapel Hill was far from a one-man show.

So many good ball players were available that many lettermen of past years gave up in disgust. They were either overlooked in the rush or foresaw the ultimate result of bench confinement.

Ends were four deep. On the left side there was Weiner, Joe Romano, Ken Powell and the remarkable Tandy. The other side could call on George Sparger, Cox, Mike Rubish and Dan Logue.

harlie was a picture-book punter

Ernie Williamson and Len Szafaryn were the starting tackles. Both were later successes in pro ball. Guards could move and had savvy. Emmett Cheek, later an assistant coach under Jim Tatum; Sid Varney, the Elon mentor who went unbeaten in 1957; Bob Mitten, and Ralph Strayhorn were standouts.

Chan Highsmith, injured in the Virginia game and sidelined for the Sugar Bowl, was a center capable of playing for anyone. Joe Wright and Don Hartig split most of the quarterbacking duty—and could "rack 'em." Camp, Jack Fitch and E. K. Grow gave wing a fine combination of runners. Good performers like Billy Myers, Johnny Clements and Bill Maceyko had to wait their turn in the backfield.

The fullbacks, however, were the ones who did the most to make Charlie a threat. Pupa and Hosea Rodgers were rugged 190-pounders with experience behind them. They delighted in charging the middle, but they had another offensive threat that threw havoc into foes. They could pass.

Snavely took full advantage of this attribute.

Pupa or Rodgers might spin and hit the line. They might spin and pass. They might spin and hand off to Justice—who might run or pass. The defense was never given a breather.

Justice, who won his service plaudits by playing the T formation, was completely at home as a tailback in Snavely's single wing. The formation called for all of his talents and it made the quick kick, one of his finest maneuvers, a tremendous weapon for the Tar Heels.

"I always get a laugh when I see I was called a ball player who needed no coaching when I arrived at Carolina," said Justice. "There is no football player who can't take coaching. I was sold from the beginning on Coach Snavely. He taught me plenty.

"We were never real close, none of that father-and-son type thing, but I had immense respect for the man. We never had a harsh word. He had a brilliant football mind."

Newspapermen, looking back on the successful 1946 season and the lesson learned in the Sugar Bowl, began calling 1947 the year of plenty for the Tar Heels. Pupa and Rodgers would be back. Justice was an oldtimer . . . a sophomore.

Lettermen for all positions were as thick as co-eds on the campus.

Snavely had to agree, although he was to lose several key men he had counted upon, that the next fall could be the finest in the history of North Carolina football.

Of course the old saw, "We'll be better but so will our opposition," was put to use.

Justice was happy at Chapel Hill and treated well. His prominence never seemed to affect his personal behavior. Fraternities courted him and he pledged Beta Theta Pi.

The first year could have been a difficult one for the touted Choo Choo. It wasn't. He fitted the campus as a student and an athlete.

27

Pigskin Professor" Kay Kyser and a couple of recruits

The thing Charlie remembered most about his glamorous frosh beginning was not the cheers, the honors, the touchdowns. It was the two kicks blocked on him by Virginia Tech. He vowed he would make amends.

Justice kicked 249 times during his collegiate career, from that fateful September, 1946, until the windup in the Cotton Bowl game on January 2, 1950. He spent hours perfecting a quick motion, polishing his timing. The extra effort was worth it, for no other kicks were blocked during his collegiate career.

IV

FIRST OF MANY TOUCHDOWNS

Winters are cold in Asheville. It is a dry, wind-cutting kind of cold that rides in on gusty breezes from the high hills and knifes deep down inside you.

It comes quickly, bitterly when darkness falls and the sun suddenly ducks behind Beaucatcher Mountain and day is ended.

And a thin, loose-limbed young boy pulls a jacket tightly around his shoulders, darts from a football dressing room, and runs cleverly, expertly past night shadows homeward.

* * * * * *

THE CHRISTMAS rush was always an exciting time of the year for young Charlie Justice.

It meant that the streets of Asheville would be crowded—and there was no better place in the world, reasoned the youngster with growing athletic ambitions, to practice his fakes and spins.

Picturing Charlie in those days brings to mind the Artful Dodger of Charles Dickens' *Oliver Twist*. It was the Dodger, at the insistence of Fagin, who pilfered packages, then outraced pursuit through the streets of London. Charlie became an honest Dodger.

He fancied himself carrying a football, with the milling shoppers the defense. Up and down Asheville's sloping streets he would gallop, coming as near to amazed strangers as he would dare.

Many a lady with a bag packed with toys and groceries shut her eyes and awaited impact with the wild-looking kid charging in her direction. Little did she know she was a practice dummy helping to develop one of the most elusive runners in the history of football.

"It got so bad," admitted Charlie, "the police began to watch for me. All of them knew me as 'that crazy kid who's always running the blocks.'"

Charlie Justice was born on May 18, 1924. He was one of a family of six sons and a daughter born to Nell Foster and Parley Wittington Justice. His father worked for the railroad, and the family knew its share of hard times during Charlie's youth. One of his brothers died in childhood from diphtheria.

"When I was growing up," says Charlie, "we moved so much I began to think everyone rented houses by the month, then vacated. I didn't grow up on the wrong side of the tracks, but we kids always had reason to believe that what money there was in the world was on the other side." In the early days, there were no electric lights in the Justice household.

Living in the country, just far enough away from Asheville to make the city seem a fairyland, Charlie didn't get the feel of a football until he was 12 years old. He recalls his first game—as a spectator—at the age of seven.

"It was eight miles to the field where they played," said Charlie. "I was too little to walk all the way, so brother Jack carried me when I gave out."

In his early years, Charlie attended schools which featured basketball and baseball, but did not participate in football because of the expense. It didn't matter. Young Justice was too small and would have been chased from the lot.

"I guess I might be referred to as the 'girl' of the Justice brothers," he candidly admits. "The older boys were athletically inclined and were on the go. My sister left home at an early age. I was always helping Mom — sweeping, ironing, washing dishes. No one thought I'd ever take to sports."

The Justices moved to Biltmore, a suburb of Asheville, when Charlie was approaching his teens, and the transfer changed his life. He felt a football for the first time. It was love at the first flight of pigskin.

The skinny, pale Charlie has been given the gift of speed and he put it to good use. The neighborhood was tough; he learned to run to stay healthy. No one could catch him in games on the back lots, so soon he became a leader of the rinkydinks.

"We'd challenge the rich kids to pickup games," said Charlie. "There was a lot of satisfaction in beating them. We never lost."

The name Justice blazed into prominence long before he entered the university at Chapel Hill. Actually, Charlie's high school career was packed with the same glitter of accomplishment as that of his college, service, and pro football.

30

Even black cats couldn't stop boyish Cha..
when he started his high school car..

At the age of 14, Choo Choo was ready for Lee Edwards High, but a ruling by the school board forced him to return to David Millard Junior High to play. He was a natural from the start, although he had virtually no background.

An early newspaper photograph from the *Asheville Citizen* featured a pink-cheeked, somewhat bewildered Charlie, posed in a stance that violated all rules of proper posture. The caption read: "Another Justice is coming along and this one is Charlie. Only last week he intercepted an aerial and ran 99 yards to give his David Millard team a 13-7 victory over Charlotte's Piedmont Junior High."

By the time Justice was a high school junior, Coach Ralph James at Lee Edwards High had moulded one of the great teams in North Carolina schoolboy history. Justice was hitting his stride. He scored 19 touchdowns in the Fall of 1941.

The next year he was even stronger. He made 27 scoring jaunts—as well as being an outstanding passer and punter. What's more, when Justice rested, a dazzling speedster named Billy Britt stepped in. They were known as the touchdown twins. For two years the Justice-led Asheville team was unbeaten during regular-season play.

The ability of the team in Charlie's senior year, when he rode to All-Southern honors and was tabbed the finest schoolboy player in Asheville's history, was evaluated by the late, respected Scoop Latimer of the *Greenville* (S. C.) *News*:

"The biggest and best high school team this corner has seen is the Asheville Maroons, who should apply for membership in the Southeastern college conference, where they might find competition. Clad in scarlet jerseys the Tar Heel hefties looked all the world like a forest fire burning their way around and over the lighter Greenville Raiders here last night, 55-0. In size, power, and capabilities the Asheville team would be superior to many college outfits.

"The Maroons reminded us of Wallace Wade's old Red Elephants of Alabama Rose Bowl fame in physique and to some extent in general deportment in style of play. We hardly expect to see more avoirdupois on the human chassis in the Georgia-Alabama game next Saturday.

"If Asheville isn't acclaimed national champions, there ain't no justice—except Asheville's own great Charlie Justice."

Asheville had a fantastic record during the fall of 1942. The team scored more than 400 points, holding the opposition to a paltry six.

One of the games was against Hickory High, and the score was 94-0. Justice had scoring runs of 21, 85, 22, and 92 yards. Britt, who later attended North Carolina but quit football in college, scored five times during the game to out-tally Choo Choo.

As the regular season ended, Paul Jones, once associated with professional baseball in Asheville but then a reporter covering the feats of Justice, interviewed the late and beloved Herman Hickman, at the time an assistant coach at North Carolina State.

32

Herman, who was later to become head coach at Yale and a radio and television personality as well as a football analyst for *Sports Illustrated*, had watched the Maroons in several games.

Said the 300-pound Hickman: "Long before I saw the team I knew it must be great and that Charlie Justice was a fine back. I just had to see some games in person to convince myself.

"I was amazed in more ways than one. Justice is a fabulous runner, and it's no longer a mystery why he rips off yardage. It's too bad that such a team had to come along at a time when we're at war.

"I may have seen at some time or other a better high school team than Asheville—but I can't remember one. And if I ever saw a better all-around high school back than Justice I can't recall the performance."

Justice and Asheville's outstanding end, Carl Tipton, were invited to play in the Shrine game at Charlotte on December 5, 1942. It was fitting that Ralph James was head coach of the Tar Heel outfit.

From the first day of practice, the visiting critics pointed to North Carolina and rated them far superior to Speedy Speer's prep stars from the Palmetto State. The prediction held.

Justice scored three times as the Tar Heels romped to a one-sided, 33-0, victory on a wet field.

Wrote Jake Wade, then sports editor of *The Charlotte Observer*: "Justice and Tipton were plenty football players yesterday. Justice just ran in stride, scooting on scrimmage plays when the chips were down, a dozen yards here, fourteen there, twenty-four for a touchdown, and when he shipped those passes so smartly, with Tipton catching them like a DiMaggio and then churning on ahead, once with a tackler on his shoulder, the rooting section from Asheville was all grin, a mile wide."

The afternoon that Justice equaled the Shrine Bowl all-time scoring mark (18 points—first achieved in 1938 by Charlie's brother, Bill Justice), *The Charlotte News* sports editor, Ray Howe, selected his All-State team for North Carolina.

Charlie was named team captain.

Three other athletes received mentions. Ernie (Bear) Knotts, later to matriculate at Duke, was on the first team. Lou Allen, Duke bound, and Wade Walker, who attended Oklahoma under Bud Wilkinson, had to be content with a second string mention. All received All-American notices as collegians.

While the Justice legend at Asheville had its story-book qualities, there were some setbacks. After the 1941 season, a charity game was arranged with Atlanta's Boys High, a dashing team led by an equally swashbuckling halfback named Clint Castleberry. The weather was excellent for crops, swimmers, and amphibious landings, and a disappointing turnout of 4,000 sat in the rain at Ponce de Leon park to watch what was billed as a game for the Southern championship. Asheville was

33

smashed in a strange affair, 44-0. Castleberry, later an All-American performer at Georgia Tech and a rare athlete who met his death during service, ran wild. Justice, too, had his moments, as Asheville gained 189 yards and outpointed the unbeaten Atlanta team in first downs, 10-7.

After the Shrine Bowl victory in 1943, James took his crack Asheville eleven to Miami for another charity affair. This time the game was played in the Orange Bowl against Miami High, coached by a barrel-chested, booming-voiced perfectionist named Jesse Yarborough.

Miami shattered Asheville's dream of a spotless record with a 13-7 triumph as a lad named Arnold Tucker, a West-Point bound quarterback who made All-American in the Blanchard-Davis era, scored twice for the Stingarees.

Justice, however, wasn't overlooked.

Praised Captain Bruce Smith of Miami, destined for high honors himself as a collegian: "Justice was as fine a back as we faced all year. He did everything well."

Justice, as a high school back, had marked himself for greatness. Colleges began persuasive courting, but Uncle Sam had a better line.

"Fellow at the draft board asked me which branch of the service I'd prefer," said Charlie. "I told him I couldn't swim and had better get in the Army—so the next thing I knew I was in the Navy."

Charlie entered the service eager to please. He forgot his high school clippings and reminded no one that he had been a standout.

The level-headed attitude, which was apparent throughout his career, dates to a dressing-down he never forgot. It came after his first role as a halfback in junior high school.

"I was in my early teens and plenty impressionable," recalls Charlie. "I got my chance in a football uniform and it seemed all too easy. The holes were there and I could run. I carried the ball three times and scored twice.

"That night, I was hustling down to our favorite hangout, a drug store as it is in most towns. I was feeling good and I knew there would be a lot of jokes and laughs and talk about football. I turned a corner and bumped into Jack."

The older brother looked at young Charlie scornfully.

"And where are you going?" he asked with obvious sarcasm. "I'll bet you're going to the drug store, to stand out in front and play big shot."

Charlie shrugged his shoulders.

"Let me tell you something, boy," said Jack. "You can go down there and blow steam if you want to. But I watched you play today. You may have scored twice, but you're the worst looking football player I ever saw. You forget about being a hero and start learning a little something about the game. You'll be a lot better off."

Charlie's father and his first Choo Choo

Young Justice looked toward the drug corner, which had already enlisted a sprinkling of evening "cowboys," and looked at Jack.

"Let's go home," he said.

V

THEY CALLED HIM CHOO CHOO

Bainbridge.

As far as the eye could see—just Navy. Boot camp. Indoctrination, drills, shots and homesickness.

On the first weekend pass, a honky-tonk studio and a portrait for Sarah and Mom back home. A photo of an eager, round-faced kid in a new uniform.

Just another Navy gob for a while. Never a Halsey, but they remember him just the same. They remember him as a special kind of Navy hero, a boot who played with men and beat them at their own game.

* * * * * *

WHEN Bainbridge Naval Training Station issued a call for football players in late summer of 1943, an early-bird candidate was a 5-10, 165-pounder named Charlie Justice.

He was one of 100, many of the others being pros and ex-college stars, and he had sufficient nerve to push toward the front of the line for choice equipment.

"You there," snapped a hardened Chief. "Where do you think you're going."

"I'd like to draw some shoes and pads," said Charlie.

"Okay, okay," growled the old warhorse, "but go to the rear of the line, sonny. We got some men we got to fit before the sea scouts take it all."

38

It brought a big laugh.

Justice moved. Half-an-hour later, he was back.

"You again?"

"Yup," sighed Charlie.

"Not yet, sonny, not yet."

On the third time around, some of the coaches nodded and Justice was offered some ill-fitting practice togs. He asked about shoes.

"We're all out," said the Chief. "Looks like you don't get to play this year."

"Doesn't matter about the shoes," said Charlie. "Where I come from in North Carolina people go barefooted most of the time anyway."

Charlie dressed in his makeshift uniform and appeared on the field carrying his socks. Lt. Joe Maniaci, who had won fame at Fordham and with the Chicago Bears, was coach. He had the kind of experienced roster that would have held its own against any team in the country.

"What do you want, young fellow?" asked Maniaci, almost laughing when he saw the barefoot boy with fuzzy cheeks.

"I'm a halfback," answered Charlie, embarrassed by the snub he was getting, but too eager to play to desert the challenge.

"Tell you what," said Maniaci. "You go to the far end of the field and catch a few of those punts and bring them back to the kickers. You won't get hurt that way."

It was better than being cut, reasoned Charlie, although he felt much like a dog chasing a stick rather than a prospect for the team.

The next day, the Chief found a pair of sneakers to issue to the outcast from Asheville. Charlie now could do some kicking. He punted one which sailed high over Maniaci's head. The coached looked up, impressed.

"Hey, kid," he yelled.

"Yessir."

"You kick like that all the time?"

"I do better when I'm wearing football shoes," said Charlie.

"From now on, kid," emphasized Joe, "you've got the best available."

Maniaci found the 19-year-old had talent, and he decided to use him in kicking situations. Charlie badgered him for a chance to run the ball.

"These boys are killers, lad," warned the lieutenant. "You're small and haven't faced this kind of competition. Most of them make their living in peacetime by eating halfbacks your size."

When Maniaci tossed him to the hungry "tigers," they growled and clawed and snapped their teeth, but Charlie was hard to keep on the plate. He darted in and out of holes like a rabbit skidding across a river of ice with a pack of hounds in chase.

"I'll be darned; I'll be darned," mumbled Maniaci. "If I wasn't here to see it, I wouldn't believe it."

Within a week, Justice, the orphan of practices, had rocketed to the top echelon. It was a battlefield promotion, at that; the highest manner in which a man can prove himself.

The company was fast. There was Gerry Ramsey, a guard from William and Mary who had made All-American; Carl Tomasello, of the New York Giants; Carl Mulleneaux, of the Green Bay Packers; Howard Hickey, of the Cleveland Rams; Bill DeCorrevont, of Northwestern, who had been the most highly sought-after high school player in history when he was a Chicago prepster; Don Durdan, the southpaw passer who was the hero of Oregon State's 20-16 victory over Duke in the transplanted Rose Bowl of 1942, and others with dazzling reputations.

A sports writer from a metropolitan newspaper visited the base one day and was impressed with the roster of big names. He asked the coach who would most likely rate the billing of brightest star?

"Keep this between me and you," Maniaci confided, "but see 'Tiny Tim' out there?"

"Yeah. The team manager?"

"No," said Maniaci, "he's a halfback named Justice. High school boy. I figure he could be our best."

The writer did a doubletake.

As he left the field, the scribe suggested to the public relations officer: "Don't dare send Maniaci to sea. With his ideas, he's liable to put the carriers in drydock and attack the Jap navy in a canoe."

Maniaci may have been slow at offering Justice the opportunity to exhibit his wares, but he knew talent when he saw it. The problem was to use the diminutive flyer in the most effective manner. The coach decided Charlie would be a spot player.

In the first seven games, Justice, darting in and out of the lineup like a lightning bug flashing signals, peeled off seven touchdowns on runs of 45, 43, 41, 40, 33, 32, and 14 yards, and averaged better than 15 yards per carry from scrimmage.

He kicked only twice—but those boots were skyscrapers of 62 and 54 from the line of scrimmage. Playing defense occasionally, he intercepted five enemy aerials. He caught nine as an offensive player.

"He's got everything," exuded Maniaci, an exponent of the T formation. "He can run, tackle, block, and boot that ball a country mile."

Maniaci, a fullback in his player days with the Bears, went even beyond that in acclaim when Bainbridge cleaned up the 1943 schedule without a loss.

Said the coach: "Charlie Justice is the best back for his size I've ever seen. Teach him a new trick and his second try looks as if he's been doing it all his life. There has never been a more natural football player."

The 1943 season was the third time in a row that Justice went through a regu-

lar schedule without a loss. The *Associated Press* named him the service "Rookie of the Year" in the Mid-Atlantic section of the United States. Bainbridge was tabbed the No. 1 team in the nation.

It was at Bainbridge that Charlie was given the sobriquet of "Choo Choo," a label that struck the taste of fans and writers alike.

Watching Charlie break loose on a fancy cutaway, an officer in the stands remarked, "Say, that Justice kid runs just like a choo-choo train."

During the height of his career as a collegian at North Carolina, Charlie became so well known he often got mail from various parts of the country addressed simply to "Choo Choo, North Carolina."

The 1944 season was even more lucrative for Justice and his famed Bainbridge mates—with names such as Lou Sossomon, the great center from South Carolina; Fullback Harvey (Stud) Johnson, of William and Mary; Halfback Harry (Hippity) Hopp, of Nebraska; Dewey Proctor, of Furman; and others to swell the roster with class.

Typical Justice tricks were seen in the game against Maxwell Field, a highly-regarded outfit, in which the Bainbridge Commodores won their 12th straight over a two-fall span, 15-7.

A Navy publication had this to say: "Justice accounted for both Commodore touchdowns, prevented a second Maxwell score when he hauled down Johnny Clements, former Chicago Cardinal, after a 73-yard breakaway, and did about everything else but tote the water bucket."

Charlie treasures a bit of conversation more than the clipping.

Len Aiken, an ex-Baylor star who had ten years of experience with the Chicago Bears, walked to the dressing room with Justice, which Charlie considered a high honor in itself. Said Aiken: "Kid, I've seen and played a lot of football, but that was about the greatest individual performance I ever hope to witness."

Bainbridge, with a line regarded as the nation's finest and a backfield of dashing performers, again was unbeaten. Justice scored 84 points and picked up 629 yards rushing.

The conscientious, vigilant *Associated Press* found itself with a problem. The year 1944 has been a good one for service elevens, particularly individuals who performed in spectacular fashion.

At 20, Justice was deserving, but he was still unknown to the masses of readers across the country. A back with only a high school background had no right to outpoint proven pro and college stars. Charlie earned a second team berth.

The first All-Service club found Otto Graham (Northwestern) of North Carolina Pre-Flight, Charlie Trippi (Georgia) of Third Air Force, Bill Dudley (Virginia) of Randolph Field, and Len Eshmont (Fordham) of Norman Navy rating the top four spots.

they said he ran like a Choo Choo at Bainbridge

The second backfield was composed of Indian Jack Jacobs (Oklahoma) of the 4th Air Force, Glenn Dobbs (Tulsa) of 2nd Air Force, Bill Daley, the Michigan All-American stationed at Fort Pierce, and Choo Choo.

Huffed *The Bainbridge Mainsheet*, official publication of the base: "If you ask us, the second string backfield is better than the first."

How good were the Bainbridge teams of Maniaci? There's no way to gauge accurately, since few opponents had the strength to really test them.

"We'll play anybody in the country, anybody in the world," bragged Lt. Joe.

There was one scrimmage with the Washington Redskins which meant nothing on the schedule, but offered a test of merit. Bainbridge was in there all the way—and ex-prep schooler Justice scampered up and down the field with his usual disregard for top brass of the grid.

"He could play for a pro team right now," predicted Maniaci.

George Marshall of the 'Skins agreed. He got word to Charlie that he'd be proud to have his name on a contract the minute he was released from service.

Two years at Bainbridge was the limit for such stars as Justice. The heat was on.

Wrote Shirley Povich, in *The Washington Post*: "Choo Choo Charlie Justice and his marauding on the gridiron practically amounted to a home front for the Navy —Halsey, Nimitz and Justice shared the headlines.

"In fact, Justice's fame was so embarrassing to the Navy that he was shipped to Honolulu during the period when Manpower Boss James M. Byrne was prodding the armed services to get their big-name athletes out of the country."

Justice had another prolific season playing with the Pearl Harbor Navy All-Stars.

He continued to keep fast company, with such names as Duke's George McAfee and Steve Lach, Minnesota's Bob Sweiger, Jackie Crain of Texas, and Lloyd Cheatham of Auburn as companions.

One of the games played was against the Marine All-Stars. Choo Choo, starting in the place of the injured McAfee, opened the way for the first touchdown with a punt return, and added several nice runs from scrimmage as the Navy triumphed, 13-0 . Star of the losing Leathernecks was a chap named Alvin Dark, later to become one of major league baseball's finest infielders.

Service football had been educational and thrilling, but Justice was ready for civilian life when the opportunity arrived. His fame had spread so far that he could have rated a ticker-tape welcome at any athletic office in the country.

Looking back on his service capers, Charlie found the most significant element was the opportunity of playing and learning football with his pro teammates.

Hopp, the Nebraska halfback, taught him the importance of using his interference at every twist and turn. In high school, the Justice speed and change of pace had been enough. Durdan, the southpaw, tipped Charlie on the importance of stay-

44

A long touchdown run even made the Gray Fox sm
(PHOTO BY BUGS BARRING

ing within the protective pocket while seeking a pass receiver. The "kid" was a good student. He never forgot the smallest detail.

It was with this immense background that Justice departed the Navy. It is little wonder that the nation's colleges wooed him. Aye, the professionals, too.

"He's equal to a pro right now," commented one coach. "Calling him a freshman football player when he enters college is like calling Joe Louis a promising young fighter."

Charlie thus became the most highly discussed talent ever to pass from high school to college, via a three-year layoff at Uncle Sam's training grounds. DeCorrevont earned a reputation in the Big Ten area during his high school jaunts in Chicago in the late 1930's, but Choo Choo was the finished product.

His choice of North Carolina gave the Chapel Hill school its most prized frosh since 1941. That was the year a big bruiser named Felix (Doc) Blanchard enrolled.

Perhaps Charlie evened the score. The service took Doc away, enrolled him at West Point where he became a three-time All-American as a fullback. Now it gave Justice in return.

VI

BEST OF THEM ALL

The lineup was impressive.

A roll call of football greatness.

They had everything: speed, experience, desire, attitude, and brawn.

"Coach Snavely's biggest problem," said a wiseacre, "is deciding which All-American to start."

It wasn't quite that easy, and the Tar Heels were slow getting the 1947 express rolling.

Once it was on the track, it went full throttle all the way.

* * * * * *

WHICH TEAM was mightiest during the Justice era at North Carolina? Most players and members of the coaching staff will cite the 1947 squad without hesitation.

Yet, that was the only season which wasn't concluded with a Bowl game.

And it was one in which the Tar Heels had to convince a passel of critics they weren't doing a Murphy bed and folding into obscurity.

Spring and summer had sharpened the desire for revenge. Georgia would furnish the opener and the salty sting from the Sugar Bowl still lingered in the mouths of the Tar Heels. Wally Butts and his Bulldogs had increased their winning skein to 17 straight. The contest was a press agent's dream.

There were 43,000 in Kenan Stadium that September afternoon when Coach Snavely uncovered what many assumed would be the "finest edition since he began coaching." Everything was present: size, depth, maturity, poise—and a demanding schedule.

The Bulldogs came out growling. Butts, masterful at preparing a defense to stymie individual talent, had Choo Choo on his list again. Whenever Charlie got the ball, red shirts multiplied like bunnies from a top hat.

At halftime, the warriors wearing blue, and those in gold and red trudged wearily off the field. It has been 30 minutes of bruises, jarring collisions, and piles of manpower stacked like Pyramids—but no one had crossed the goal.

A rotund man, far beyond the years of cheerleading, led the Tar Heels back on the field after their rest. His name was Lath Morris. To thousands of North Carolina followers he was known as "Tarzan," and he could be described as a 300-pound character.

Perspiring freely, Tarzan held a megaphone to his lips and shouted, "Go, go, go, go, go . . . Care-lina!"

The students chanted back, "Go, go, go, go . . . Tarzan!"

The woolly Rameses, usually grouchy and unconcerned, seemed to take to the spirit of the cheer. He pulled at his chain. The Snavely machine suddenly came to life.

Justice remained a threat—one sure touchdown pass he tossed was dropped, the receiver all alone. But the steady Walt Pupa was in the bullpen, and he unlimbered his arm with scoring heaves to Ends Cox and Weiner. Air power resulted in a 14-7 victory.

"Our defense was big," reasoned Snavely at the conclusion. "Why, anytime you limit a passer like Georgia's Johnny Rauch to four completions in 13 tries, you're really doing a job. I just hope we can do the same to Bobby Layne next week at Texas."

Bobby Layne. Texas. Little did Snavely realize his team was to be jolted like an aspiring cowpoke riding a Brahma bull for the first time.

The airplane ride to Austin was a chamber of horrors to the Tar Heels. Rough weather was encountered from the beginning. Justice, as well as more than half the squad, wore a green coating of nausea hours before landing time.

The next morning, the sun came up Texas style, big and demanding. What the boys would have given to stay in their hotel rooms and listened to the World Series. The afternoon before, Cookie Lavagetto's hit with two away in the ninth had robbed New York's Floyd Bevans of a no-hitter, and had won for Brooklyn, 3-2, in the opening game.

It was baseball weather—for a football menu.

Early in the first period, Quarterback Layne, later to become one of pro football's most adroit passers and runners, hit Halfback Bryon Gillroy for a touchdown. The Tar Heels couldn't match the pace.

It was 20-0 at halftime, and Carolina stalwarts were dropping as if drugged. Guard Bob Mitten blacked out three times before finally being benched. Final score: 34-0.

Justice had one of his most disappointing days, before 47,000 people. His chief contribution was an average of 47.6 on five punts.

"We didn't have it," sighed Snavely. "We just didn't have it."

"We have Layne—you keep Choo Choo," chanted the Texas cheering section.

The die-hards blamed it on the disturbing trip into the Lone Star State and the insufferable heat, Wake Forest would bring a recovery in clean, fresh air, they prophesied.

Peahead Walker's limited but amply-muscled legions came to Kenan unbeaten and left the same way the following weekend. At the mid-point, the Deacs were leading by a startling 19 points, and it took a Justice toss to End Danny Logue, a one-time Notre Dame recruit who had transferred to Chapel Hill, to save a blanking.

Choo Choo got off a quick kick for 79 yards, one of his best, but Tom Fetzer and Bud Lail passed the Tar Heels into a state of shock.

"We were outclassed," mused Snavely. "There's something missing this year . . ."

Justice, emotionally upset, looked at the walls of the dressing room and sighed, "We've got nothing left but our press clippings."

But the turmoil had just begun.

Charlie went to the coach the next Monday and asked for a confidential chat.

"I hate to bring this up," said the little halfback, "but I've heard talk that our team isn't getting 100 per cent effort. If I'm the cause, I regret it.

"Publicity can be bad—and I know I've had more than my share. Maybe the others feel they're being overlooked. If it will help the team, don't start me."

Snavely pondered a moment. Then he said, "Charlie, we might have to move you from the No. 1 backfield for another reason."

Pic Magazine, now defunct, had carried a story that week with Charlie as its cover boy. Dave Camerer, a former Dartmouth tackle, had done the writing—and had mentioned rumors of Justice having signed a contract with the Philadelphia Eagles while at Bainbridge.

The Southern Conference, of which North Carolina was a member, questioned Charlie's eligibility.

As if Snavely and his comrades weren't having enough troubles!

William and Mary was the foe the next Saturday at Richmond—but Charlie wasn't to be given a clean bill of health until minutes before game time, just like in the old-time serials.

There actually had been a move by the Eagles to land Justice as a teen-ager, but Elmer Layden, then Commissioner of the pro league and one of the original Notre Dame Four Horsemen, had ruled, "The Navy boy is too young to be signed in this league. There is no such thing as a contract."

Carolina got Justice and itself back on level ground the same day. Charlie, breathing easier, made 55 yards on 17 tries, and pitched to Wingback Jim Camp for two touchdowns. It meant a 13-7 victory over the Indians.

"Jim," said Charlie to the scoring ace of the day, "you played a great game out there. You were the best man on the field."

Said Camp: "This team is going places. We're just beginning to play the kind of football expected of us."

Florida was next and that prediction held. Justice scored one time in a 35-7 rout of the 'Gators at Gainesville, but a wild horse appeared in the form of Fullback Hosea Rodgers. His marks were astounding.

"Hosey," as he was called by his mates, carried eight times for 112 yards, then completed six of 10 passes for 126 additional yards. The Justice score was a 76-yard run, following a lateral from the dashing fullback.

Carolina's record was 3-2. The bandwagon was gaining riders.

Snavely was in a jovial mood that Sunday as he sat in the den of his handsome, spacious home on Tenney Circle. He enjoyed eating ice cream in big helpings as he reviewed film clips of the team's progress.

"I've got a personal challenge coming up when Tennessee visits here in a few days," he said. "I've never been beaten by a coach three times in a row—and General Neyland of the Vols trimmed me our last two meetings. I'd like to pay him back some of the anguish he's doled out."

The Dutchman smiled. Two weeks previous, he had wondered whether his team would recover to again become a sound unit. Disaster from individual problems was a possibility. Then came the roaring rebound.

Tennessee was always tough—but few Carolina teams in history have gone into a game with a better mental attitude. The Vols were doomed.

Justice led the attack. He scored once, passed to Cox for a second and to Tandy for a third.

"You can't ask much more of a player than Justice gave today," said an exhilarated Snavely.

"We were lucky," said Neyland in a terse comment, "that we didn't get licked worse."

The series with North Carolina State was at last revived. It had been halted during the war years because of extreme feelings between the student bodies. The Wolfpack, coached by Beattie Feathers, was on edge to stop Carolina's attack.

The game was over almost as soon as it had started.

51

Charlie and Fullback Hosea Rodgers become inseparable pals

On the first play from scrimmage, Pupa took the center pass, faked to Justice and kept the ball. Wolfpack linemen went for Choo Choo, and a hole opened the size of a walk-in vault. Pupa was in the open like a big cat.

The fullback traveled 45 yards without assistance. On the 25, a lone red-shirted defender raced to bring him down. Suddenly a Tar Heel appeared and cut the safety man from his feet. Pupa scored standing and looked back to find Justice had taken out the last man with a key block.

The score was 41-6 when the end came, and Choo Choo had been active. He carried 14 times and totaled 123 yards rushing. He completed three of four passes for 42 yards. Five punts sailed for a 41-yard mark.

Once again Snavely was all smiles. He fingered a red, white and blue tie.

"I'm not superstitious," he said, "but after losing to Texas and Wake Forest, I got this tie in the mail from a friend. I've worn it every game since and we haven't lost yet. I'm not going to take it off."

Maryland, which hadn't completed its famed Byrd Stadium, arranged for its game with the Tar Heels to be played at Washington, D. C. Jim Tatum had taken over coaching reins at College Park after departing Oklahoma, and the matching of wits between the crafty, energetic South Carolinian, in opposition to his former teacher, King Carl, captured the fancy of the public.

Strong, capable Pupa had to prove himself as durable as the lone burro in a gold rush in this one. Tatum's defenses were rigged to halt Choo Choo and were effective. The fullback accepted the brunt of the attack, carried a back-breaking 32 times. Justice scored once, as the Tar Heels finished forcibly with three touchdowns in the fourth quarter and a 19-0 triumph.

The billing when the annual tea party with Duke arrived was: Charlie Justice vs. Fearless Freddie Folger—a battle of single wing tailbacks.

Folger excelled in one department, punting, when he compiled a 43.3 average to Charlie's even 40. But North Carolina defenses, led by colorful Earthquake Smith, were rigged with spikes. Folger carried nine times, gained but six yards.

Choo Choo was ablaze. His running was a limited 34 yards for 13 tries, but he was a Bob Feller on the mound, with seven completions in 11 attempts. He scored twice, and passed for another touchdown in Duke's famed horseshoe stadium.

Final score: UNC 21, Duke 0.

Said Wallace Wade: "They simply beat us down as deep as they are." It was the worst licking Duke had taken from its Chapel Hill foe since the "team of 1,000 backs" had done the mauling, 38-7, in 1929.

The Tar Heels were back in the national limelight after their substantial showing of power against their No. 1 rival. Chapel Hill was a midway of noisy demonstrations, singing and snake dancing.

A small party of conservative Tar Heels arrived at the Carolina Inn several

53

ven on the sidelines, he was the most exciting person in the stadium

hours after game time and was disappointed to find the dining room closed. The early evening had been spent in conversation; time had slipped up on them.

James Weaver, a colored employee of the Inn, seemed as disturbed as the would-be customers that the chain had been pulled. He excused himself to seek the manager.

"Sir," began James, "we just got to open up that dining room again."

"We can't, James," replied the manager. "Rules are rules. It's far beyond closing time."

"But you got the most important man in North Carolina standing out there goin' hungry."

"Do you mean to tell me Governor Cherry is in the lobby?"

"Oh, no, Sir, not anybody like that. I mean the MOST important — Mr. Charlie (Choo Choo) Justice."

Dinner was served!

A crowd of 40,000 flooded Kenan Stadium for the finale with Virginia. The Tar Heels were at their peak—large, bold, and sassy.

Justice ran wild, with 152 yards on 12 carries, one of them for a touchdown. He scored a second touchdown on a sensational catch of a Rodgers pass. It was a 40-7 windup.

"Best club we've seen all year," stated Art Guepe, coach of the Cavaliers.

Frank Thomas, ailing and receiving treatment at Duke Hospital, had been a guest on the Tar Heels' bench that day. Said the former Alabama coach: "I've seen quite a few teams in my time—but none was smoother than the North Carolina club I saw today. It had everything."

Bowl invitations arrived like telephone calls to the prettiest girl on the block.

No less than nine, ranging from the insignificant to the highly flattering and lucrative, were considered.

In Los Angeles, a promotional group which had already sold some $10,000 worth of tickets on an overnight idea, promised in excess of $100,000 for the Tar Heels to make an appearance for a late December game.

An organization in Boston said it would devise its own Bowl and present a blank check if Snavely and Company would strut in Beantown. The Orange Bowl was rejected when it could not guarantee the Tar Heels tickets to satisfy the needs of alumni and backers.

It seemed hard to believe. Two months earlier, the Tar Heels had been their own worst enemy. Now they were everybody's heroes.

The official *Associated Press* rating listed UNC 10th in the nation.

Justice was named the Most Valuable Player in the Southern Conference and placed on the *AP*'s second All-America team, a notch higher than his freshman accolade.

always turned it on when he turned the corner

The Tar Heels, after a lengthy discussion, decided against Bowl participation and put their offense in mothballs, along with Coach Snavely's good-luck red, white and blue neckpiece.

Despite the early heartbreaks, it had been a great season.

VII

WHAT MADE CHARLIE RUN

No one completely explained it. Not satisfactorily. His ability defied words.

On the field, he was a slippery eel, elusive, dangerous, thrilling to watch. He utilized all the tricks—the feints, the cutbacks, the timing, the stiff-arm, pace changing.

Like watching a magician, one appreciated the result, didn't question the method.

Droll, slow-talking Douglas Clyde Walker, then master of Wake Forest's legions, put it this way:

"Justice—he reminds me of a beautiful woman. Everybody's reaching out to grab—and it looks like it won't be too difficult. Just when you get your confidence up, you get the slip and are left there standing all alone."

* * * * * *

THE FRESHMAN football squad stood on the sidelines at Navy Field and watched a Monday dummy scrimmage. The Saturday game had been grueling, but perfectionist Carl Snavely wanted to test a few plays against a Tennessee defense.

Shadows had fallen over most of the campus and a six o'clock quietness floated over the crisp, autumn scene. The chimes of the Bell Tower would soon be heard.

Charlie Justice was running at tailback. Joe Wright was at blocking back. Jim Camp was the wingback and Hosey Rodgers commanded fullback.

"Charlie," advised Backfield Coach Crowell Little, "hit in that hole just a half step faster. That's what is wrong."

On the next play Justice followed Little's advice and reached the secondary until he was spilled by Johnny Clements. A whistle blew.

"Gosh," said a young kid from Shelby, "there's nobody in the world like Choo Choo."

"Listen, buddy," his brash teammate said, "he puts on his pants just like you and me."

"Yeah," said the awed frosh, "but when he gets *his* on—something different happens."

Justice was the ideal player. He was relaxed, yet determined. He loved the game, he relished contact, he liked to practice.

He was no saint in daily workouts. He did his share of horsing around, but there was little you could get away with under Snavely, Reed, Russ Murphy, Little, Jim Gill, and the other Tar Heel coaches.

The one thing that set him apart from most All-American prima donnas was that Justice was a team player. He blocked and he played well on defense. Coach Murphy once said Justice could have been one of the game's finest defensive players— particularly against passes—despite his size. Even during his heyday at Chapel Hill, he saw plenty of action as a defender.

One of the criticisms of Snavely was the "risks" some thought he took with Charlie. He worked him hard in practice and ran him often. Fans visualized Justice on brilliant end sweeps, yet he ate up yardage between tackles, where elbows and fists flew. He moved up fast on defense and threw his 160-170 pounds at hard-charging fullbacks without hesitation. This from a halfback who was billed as a triple-threat on offense.

During a coaches' clinic one summer in the late 1940's, a group had gathered to discuss football in informal fashion. A high school tutor brought up the name Justice and said he felt the halfback was used too much when conditions didn't warrant it.

"I recall when North Carolina played Virginia," he said. "Justice was still in the game with a three-touchdown lead. Is that smart? Why take chances?"

Said Rube McCray of William and Mary: "When a back was going like Justice was going against Virginia that particular afternoon he belongs just one place— out there on the field."

Mental attitude had much to do with Justice's success. Before each game he was nervous and edgy, as have been many of the great actors of the stage. He was superstitious. Before the Texas game in 1948, he had a rabbit's foot sewn into his pants lining.

On the way to another touchdow

On the sidelines, he built his emotion. He was restless, jumped about to the point of becoming an exhibitionist. He was more active than most cheerleaders, his high-pitched voice easily distinguishable on the field as he yelled encouragement to his colleagues.

But once he lined up and got the feel of the football, he became all business. The outside world did not exist. The battle was the thing.

There were moments when relations were strained with some members of the squad, but these were few. In one spring scrimmage game, Charlie got the roughhouse treatment and bristled on two occasions. The incident was no more than sailors seeing too much of each other on submarine duty and blowing steam.

The Tar Heel squad had players logging hours on the bench who would have been regulars on most college teams. Few resented the fact they were second and third stringers. No one honestly could challenge the worth of Justice.

Charlie had come to play. He had a burning desire for success, far stronger than his competitors. There was a fierce, almost unnatural quest to win every game.

Choo Choo wasn't billed on many losing marquees. In his high school, service, and college career, he was a member of teams which won 76, tied twice, and lost but 10.

He maintained superb conditioning rather effortlessly throughout his career. He had little tendency toward becoming overweight. He didn't smoke, and had firm convictions against drinking.

There was no blinding speed in the legs of Charlie Justice. He was fast, but his mastery at change-of-pace brought him his column of touchdowns. His head and shoulder fakes, coupled with fluid hip movements, fooled the opposition from the first day he ran in practice.

Alert, waspish Tom Anderson, of the *Knoxville Journal,* watched Charlie's 74-yard scoring spin against the Tennessee Volunteers in 1946 and sat down to chart it in words. Wrote Tom:

"Before the season began, a majority of football writers everywhere promised themselves they would go easy on superlatives. After all, a war has just been fought and won and it will be very silly, indeed, for us to be calling mere players of the game 'great' . . . 'splendid' . . . 'magnificent' . . . 'incomparable' . . . and so forth.

"But what, now we ask, in the devil, are you going to use for words to describe young lunks like Charlie Justice even half-adequately? You simply cannot do it without resorting to the stereotyped superlatives because he is undoubtedly one of the greatest ball carriers of all time.

"While Justice probably has every tackle-avoiding trick in the book, we thought his ability to stop dead, skip out of the way of charging defenders and then resume his trip in a new direction was the most effective maneuver. Besides seeing some outstanding football games this fall, I have had the additional privilege and pleas-

60

ure of watching the best passer and best runner in the South. They would be Harry Gilmer of Alabama and Justice. Of the two, we would take Justice for our club since we dearly love to watch those babies go with the mail."

With his movements, Justice had a gift of sight that is rare. Bob Cousy, the famed basketballer, put this gift to use. It's termed peripheral vision, and those fortunate enough to possess it have the advantage of much wider lateral perception than normal. It was not unusual to see Justice jaunt off tackle, fake to his left, cut back to his right, escape a linebacker who thought he had a "sure" shot from the blind side—without ever looking directly at the opposing charger.

He mentally "saw" the entire field. He "counted" players, knowing where most were, what they were doing. He faked his head, shoulders, and hips, often seconds before it appeared necessary to get a commitment from a player.

One coach summed it this way: "I have watched Justice carefully and I think I know what he does. All players to him are like standing tenpins. They appear upright, steady. When they make a move, he notes that movement; if they don't make a move, he will fake. That half-second when they commit themselves registers with him. He'll run at them in that instant when they are thinking—and he out-thinks them. "I know what he does, but you can't teach other players to think with him. I wish I could."

Justice was just an average student. Spanish was tough, he had trouble memorizing stones for a Geology rock quiz, and he never made Dean's list. But he progressed with his class. He had no great, burning desire for high honors, rather for the exposure of college education. He was not preparing for a career other than football—and he was a student of that art.

He was under pressure from hardened professors who were wittingly or unwittingly determined not to hold him in awe, not to impart favors.

After one particularly complex Spanish quiz, the professor returned examination papers. When he got to Charlie's, he read the mark. It was a 68.

"Mr. Justice," he said sarcastically, "how is it you can do so brilliantly on the football field but can only score a 68 on a routine Spanish quiz?"

"Well," shot back Justice, "I guess it's because I've got ten men helping me out there."

At Chapel Hill, Snavely, himself a former college professor, handed out books of plays, defenses, and notes which would have required the average student to burn the midnight oil. Justice and his teammates were undergoing two educational processes —on the football field and in the classroom.

It was not easy on any of them.

There were other pressures. He often received 200 letters a week. The University gave him little help in answering them. Sarah, who was also going to school, had limited time.

Then his son Ronnie was born, and Justice became husband, father, student, and athlete. It was not uncommon on the campus, but it was hard on the young man in whose hands the destiny of a grid empire rested.

There were those who scoffed at him, saying that he was just another "dumb athlete," but University records fail to show it. He was an average student, and, in the classroom, this was enough for Charlie. On the field—it would have killed him.

He wanted to win in a fervid kind of way, yet he was not one who doted on awards and honors.

In his senior year Justice failed to make the United Press All-American team, and some of his close friends were upset. Charlie, they said, ought to be cushioned for the shock.

One went by the halfback's home and suggested a spin in the car.

"Charlie, I've just heard about the United Press team. I hate to tell you, but you didn't make it," he said.

They rode several minutes and Charlie did not reply.

"Charlie, how do you feel about it?"

"Why, I feel the same as I did last year when I did make it," he answered, unconcerned.

There were times when the pressure showed. There are those critics who say he failed in the "big ones"—the bowl games. However, the records indicate he was actually sharper in the toughest games.

It was against traditional rivals like Duke, Tennessee, and Georgia that he romped best of all.

Before the games the headlines screamed, "Justice and Pals Face . . ." He read the papers, building up his own tension. Sarah kept a rather extensive scrapbook in which she pasted cover pictures from *Life, Collier's,* and scores of other magazines. He made the third string All-American team as a freshman and continued to move higher on the A-A squad until he graduated. There was always the fear in the hearts of the even most loyal Tar Heel fans that he would "slip." All this he knew and carried with him.

No matter what the prestige of the bowl games, Duke was always the "Big One" at Chapel Hill. Justice, under pressure of this game, thrived.

In his four years against Duke, 12 touchdowns were scored and he either scored, passed, or had a direct hand in 11 of the 12.

In the College All-Star game, Justice was the ace of them all.

Justice was a natural athlete. Perhaps this was the key. Whatever he did, he did well.

Once in Charlotte, after a long layoff, he decided to shoot a round of golf. He teed off on Charlotte's Eastwood golf course, banged a hole-in-one on the first green.

After football he returned to basketball, and played with a haphazard, screwball team called the Carolina Clowns. In high school he was a good baseball player and he played with a crack Chapel Hill softball team.

he going got rough—but never too rough

Wally Butts, the rotund and colorful Georgia coach, once admonished his team, "Watch him close. He'll outrun you, outpass you, outthink you. He'll fake you out of your shoes in a broken field. Take no chances with Justice."

This ability to outrun, outpass, outthink the opposition came naturally. And there must have been heredity attached to it.

Justice came from a family of outstanding athletes. His father, a railroad employee, was keen on Charlie's devotion to play. His mother, just the opposite, said she threatened to spike his football with an ice pick so he wouldn't cavort so much.

Mrs. Justice, a lady of the old school, felt the boys should work more and play less.

Charlie followed in his brothers' footsteps. He was early in the spotlight, but in those early years he was compared to three older brothers.

They taught him much, and he always looked upon them as the "real athletes of the family."

Jack, the oldest of the boys, played at Asheville from 1933-35. He was an outstanding halfback and also played well on the basketball squad. Jack won the North and South Carolina middleweight boxing championship in 1934. He enrolled at Rollins College, Florida, was shifted to guard, and became the terror of Florida grid circles.

Joe played at Asheville from 1934-36 and made all-state quarterback in 1935. He was an all-stater in basketball in 1936. He, too, went to Rollins, and became a Little All-American player. As a baseball player, he toured Cuba in 1939 with the All-American squad. He later coached in high school and then joined the Rollins coaching staff.

Neil Justice played at Asheville from 1941-43, but unfortunately was known as "Choo Choo's brother." He entered the Navy and finally compiled a strong record as a college athlete.

Bill Justice was another star. He played at Asheville from 1937 to 1939 and was an All-State halfback in 1938. He set the Shrine Bowl scoring record of three touchdowns that stood until tied by Charlie in 1942. He continued his career at Rollins and later turned to high school coaching.

*   *   *

For many athletes, a little conceit would have been natural. But Charlie had seen his family get a measure of fame before his day, and it had no effect on the lives of the other Justice boys. This served as a steadying influence.

Whenever letters arrived, or wires from devoted fans like Claudia Canady of Chapel Hill, he was always a little surprised, as he was when people recognized him on the street.

It was not unusual to see him hurrying across the campus, his short, shuffling steps carrying him at almost a trot, with his eyes watching his feet as if afraid to look up. The fame, the notoriety, the whispered "there goes Choo Choo," embarrassed him.

65

He wrestled with this discomfort on the campus when some youngsters went so far as to call him "Mr. Justice." He didn't know how to cope with it, so he stuck closely to his married friends like Rodgers, Ted Hazelwood, and others. Their kidding and ribbing relaxed him.

He was frankly impressed with his teammates and tried to push them into the limelight. It was hard to do, for no matter how publicized some were, it was Justice everyone wanted to meet and speak to.

He liked to talk of games in terms of what "Hosey did against Florida" or "Walt's run against State." He was doubly proud of his association with other stand-out University athletes who happened to share a billing with him on the sports pages—names like Hook Dillon and Bones McKinney of basketball fame; Vic Seixas in tennis; Jimmy Thomas, the swimmer; Bill Albans, the unpredictable trackman, and the super-stylish golfing of handsome Harvie Ward.

Justice was humbled when Dr. Frank Porter Graham, the University's beloved president, waved to him during his frequent campus walks and congratulated him on a performance. He enjoyed stopping by Robert A. (Coach Bob) Fetzer's office and listening to the advice of the warm and sincere athletic director.

Coaches liked Justice, for he learned quickly and was willing to tackle any assignment. He didn't loaf, didn't come up with the old "varsity limp" to duck practice, seldom suited out in sweat clothes when hard scrimmages were ordered.

"Charlie is a player's player," a teammate once said.

There could be no higher tribute.

VIII

KENAN STADIUM ALAMO

It was a time for cheering.

Even the cheerleaders followed tradition at the University. There was energetic Vic Huggins who introduced the mascot called Rameses; and a jumping-jack named Kay Kyser who clowned throughout his career; and a little guy named Billy Arthur who captured the hearts of thousands.

Now it was autumn again and a swimmer and diver of national prominence took over. Norm Sper, Jr. wrung every breath in Kenan Stadium and wrapped the Tar Heel loyal in a coat of happy frenzy. He had 'em sitting still long enough at halftime to put on impressive, colorful card stunts for the first time.

Yes, it was a time for cheering.

THE LADY wore elegant clothes and her fingers were cluttered with expensive rings. She was polite but concerned as she peered into the window of the press box.

"Pardon me," she said, "but I must see this game."

A writer looked up from his typewriter. He was filing a pre-game color report for his newspaper and the interruption irked him.

"Just look down there then, m'am," said the reporter, pointing to the lower section of Kenan Stadium. "It'll all take place down there in a few minutes."

67

"You don't understand," she pleaded. "I'm from Dallas. We . . . my husband and I chartered a plane this morning. We got here and there are no tickets. He's outside. The gateman allowed me to step over here."

"Sorry . . . I can't help you."

"Can't someone help me? The price doesn't matter. We must get in."

She was rich—but an admission to the pearly gates couldn't be bought.

When North Carolina kicked off to the Texas Longhorns that sunny fall afternoon to open the 1948 season, hundreds of fans milled outside the stadium offering big bills to slip past the gatekeepers.

Tickets had vanished. The aisles of Kenan were packed, a violation of normal procedure. There were tales of $250 bribes for ticket takers to turn their backs; one cigar-smoking, cowboy boot-wearing citizen of the Lone Star was said to have flashed a lease of an oil well for two good seats.

Of all the games played in Kenan Stadium's history, the Texas visit in September of 1948 was the most dramatic. The setting was ideal.

Like the Georgia invasion following the Sugar Bowl the previous year, there was a revenge motive for the Tar Heels. Both clubs were given high rankings in pre-season polls. The engagement was billed as the intersectional classic of the year, and Texans didn't want to miss it. Chapel Hill's little airport bulged with small aircraft carrying big Longhorns.

The only thing Texas won that joyous afternoon was the toss of the coin. In five minutes, 43,500 fans were either howling with wild, uninhibited joy or slumped in stunned silence. Carl Snavely's Tar Heels played football to perfection. When the curtain came down, the score was a shocking 34 to 7 in favor of the Blue and White.

Texans had smiled when it began. End Mike Rubish gave them his "poor boy" routine and kicked off barefooted, a skill he had mastered. The pigskin wobbled lazily downfield and was taken on the 10 by Halfback Billy Pyle, who returned it to the 22. The Longhorns got nowhere in their first series of plays and punted.

Charlie Justice, his legs taut like a puma ready to spring, took it on the Carolina 20; he almost broke away but finally was pulled to rest on the Texas 41. It was a 39-yard return, and all the paying guests were standing.

The Tar Heels were off to the races. A first-down pass failed, then Justice slanted off right tackle for 21 yards. Next came a surprise for the Longhorns—another first-down toss, but this one clicked to Art Weiner for a touchdown. After only 3:30 and Bob Cox's conversion, it was 7-0 in favor of Carolina.

Texas found the Tar Heel forward wall savage. Before they had a chance to recover from the initial touchdown, Snavely's men had another — the result of a fumble some two minutes later.

Late in the second half, when the game was hopelessly lost, the Longhorns called for time to use smelling salts on one of their shocked troops. A curly-haired guard for Carolina named Bill Wardle unpacked his verbal needle and tried an injection on a beefy, orange-shirted lineman.

68

"It's sure going to be a long ride back to Texas," chortled Wardle.

Pow! The remark was the breaking point. The angry Texan dispatched an uppercut off the grass and Wardle's jaw was the target. The UNC guard took an abrupt seat in the clover. Cooler heads prevailed and there was no more punching. But Wardle was right. It was a long way back to Austin.

Justice, the hero among heroes, had scored twice and regained his respect from the Texans. Every time the Tar Heels needed breathing space, Charlie's talented toe would buy it. His punting average was a thunderous 43.3 and kept the Longhorns deep in their own territory.

"The outcome amazed me," said Charlie as he pulled off his togs. "Last night I didn't think we had it in us. I was worried. Before the game, our boys had little to say. You couldn't figure it.

"But from the first tackle by Bobby Weant, I sensed something extra. We were sharp. Our moves were right. Texas players noticed it, too. It was that perfect game you're always hoping for but seldom get."

What followed the Texas spectacular was a game in which Tar Heel fans nearly had collective heart failure. But Carolina finally beat Georgia, 21-14, at Athens.

The Tar Heels ran over the Bulldogs in the first half much as they had the Texans, but the attack bogged time after time. The yardage margin was ten first downs to none—but the scores didn't come.

Georgia took the lead on an intercepted pass, and all of Justice's early efforts were wasted. A touchdown pass to Kenny Powell was nullified by a penalty, and Weiner dropped another close in.

The Tar Heels and Justice wouldn't be denied. The third period was picture-book football.

Charlie ran wild in the third as glum, shirt-sleeved Georgians grieved. Right off the bat Justice engineered a 78-yard drive that was practically flawless. Starting on his own 22, Charlie passed to Bob Kennedy for 12, Bill Flamish next for 19, cut around end on a sweep for another ten, hit Powell with a 30-yarder. The ball rested on the Georgia nine. It was fitting that the next play called for Justice off tackle, and he made it.

The Tar Heels were sizzling. Even rabid Bulldog fans had to admire the precision—the contrast being so different from the haltingly ineffective Tar Heels of the first half.

Georgia was unable to gain after the kickoff. The Bulldogs punted to the Tar Heels' 25. Then another 75-yard drive was underway, with the Choo Choo in command.

Sherman pulled in the punt and ran 30 yards to Georgia's 45. Hosea Rodgers passed to Max Cooke on the 14, a pretty 28-yarder. Justice again. Bingo! It was 14-7 after "True Toe" Cox finished his chore.

The highlight of the contest came in the fourth period. Justice snared a punt on the 16-yard line of Georgia, and set sail. He headed for the right sideline. His

teammates formed a wedge in front of him. The Bulldogs fell like soldiers in an un-marked mine field. He cut to his left and appeared to be going faster than he had ever run in his brilliant career. Only Jack Bush remained in front of him now. Would he get him?

Weiner took care of that obstacle. He mowed down Bush in tenpin fashion and fans went wild as Charlie scooted across again—the climax of an 84-yard run and his third touchdown of the afternoon.

The 84-yarder was Justice's longest all-the-way junket since his freshman year. The mob at Jack Lipman's hangout in Chapel Hill, listening on radio, demanded set-ups on the house.

"The Oldtimer," a feature of *The Atlanta Journal* written by the late O. B. Keeler, gave Justice one of his most laudatory compliments following the Georgia caper. Commented Keeler:

"Move over Frankie Sinkwich and Charley Trippi for there was a visitor to your domain who deserves at least an equal billing. After the exhibition Charlie Justice staged at Athens in leading North Carolina to a 21-14 victory over the Bulldogs, he doesn't have to take his hat off to anyone."

Next Wake Forest. And at fearful Groves Stadium. It was tough playing Peahead Walker's grim Deacons in Baptist Hollow, but the Tar Heels were up to it. They won, 28-6, before 27,000 fans, the largest turnout in the stadium's history.

Justice got his sixth touchdown of the year, picked up 76 yards in rushing, completed four of ten passes for 33 more yards, and averaged 49 yards on three punts.

But Rodgers was the workhorse. Justice was bounced hard out-of-bounds early in the game, and Tar Heel fans roared their protest. It was rough, tough foot-ball, but they didn't like it. Justice was used sparingly after that, but he did return in the third period to get off a memorable 74-yard quick kick which rolled dead on Wake's 11-yard line.

Asked about the sideline incident, crusty Coach Walker growled: "What do you expect my boys to do—watch the yard markers when they're chasing Justice? Next thing you know somebody will suggest asking his permission, like being at a dance. Heck, this is war and Justice has got most of the ammunition."

On Tuesday, students grabbed for the *Daily Tar Heel*, the bible of the campus. Headlines told the story. It appeared the world over.

Will Grimsley, *Associated Press* sportswriter, put it this way:

"NEW YORK (AP)—Oct. 12—College football's first ten underwent a reshuffling today after one of its dizziest Saturdays and the loud thump you heard was Notre Dame fall-ing off the top rung.

"The Irish, who had held the No. 1 position almost a year, were dumped to second place by North Carolina, a Dixie institution where a lad named Charlie (Choo Choo) Justice gets his higher learning."

There was joy in Chapel Hill that night. Everyone sang the song: Tar Heels No. 1, Notre Dame 2, Northwestern 3, Michigan 4, and Army 5. It was bigtime for sure, and Justice was the man who again lit the skyrocket.

e All-American check list: Wade Walker of Oklahoma (left), Dan Hill of Duke,
ttie Feathers of Tennessee, Justice and George Barclay of North Carolina

The work was far from done. Carl Snavely feared a letdown. N. C. State was coming up, and Beattie Feathers had the top defensive unit in the nation. The Wolfpack had played Duke to a scoreless tie, lost 0-6 to powerful Clemson, and walloped Davidson 40-0.

It was a bruising battle. It appeared that Justice was completely stymied at last. The Wolfpack dominated the first half, getting to the one, the one-half, the 28, the 14, and the 26-yard lines, missing a field goal, and generally playing the game in Tar Heel territory. Instead of the defensive honors going to State for slowing the Asheville Express, it was the Tar Heel stalwarts who shared honors as they stopped disaster from occurring in unhappy Kenan.

Rodgers fumbled twice, giving State good chances, and 44,000 watched painfully as he was dressed down in front of the Tar Heel bench by Snavely. It was an embarrassing afternoon. Hosea, the big, calm he-man from Alabama, atoned for the fumbles, scoring once and picking up 63 yards on the ground. Charlie got only 35, but showed he still had the touch when he heaved to Weiner from the State 49 to the 28 and the leggy Art walked a tightrope for the second touchdown. The final: Carolina 14, State 0.

The Tar Heels slipped to third in the *AP* poll and had LSU coming up. In Knoxville, however, Tennessee was fresh from a great win over Alabama—with ace J. B. Proctor injured on the sidelines—and had a breather in Tennessee Tech facing them.

General Bob Neyland, the Vols' coach, made no bones about his squad's intentions. After the Tech game, he entered the Vols' dressing room.

"How many men does it take to make a team?" he yelled.

"Eleven!" the Vols shouted back.

"Now with all due respect to J. B. (Proctor), this proves what we can do as a team—eleven."

"Eleven," repeated the fired-up Vols.

"And are we gonna take North Carolina the same way?"

"Yeahhh," thundered the massive Volunteers.

Louisiana State proved little more than a stiff workout. Charlie scored again, passed for two touchdowns, and the third and fourth stringers played the rest of the 34-7 game.

Then came the Volunteers in their own lair—Shields-Watkins Field in Knoxville.

Justice took to the air and passed the Tar Heels to a spirited, sweating 14-7 win, the sixth straight of the season and 13th in a row over two years.

The Snavelymen showed a new series of single-wing magic on the single-wing Vols. They were surprised. Justice hit Flamish with a touchdown beauty in the first period and later got Weiner in the open for a second TD pass. But the Tar Heels had to hang on to win from the determined Tennessee eleven.

73

sonal appearances were a must for Justice—and often a pleasure

The Carolina team was riding high. It looked like an undefeated season was within grasp.

William and Mary followed Tennessee, and the biggest attraction was the heralded battle between the Indians' Jack Cloud and Rodgers, both vying for all-conference and All-American honors.

The Indians came to Kenan a four-touchdown underdog. They went home with a 7-7 tie. Fumbles cost the Tar Heels dearly, and the Indians played it close to their chests. A deadlock was good enough for them on the soggy turf.

Not since 1898—a full 50 years before—had a Tar Heel team gone undefeatend and untied. Again the chance was missed. William and Mary was soundly beaten except in score. They were outgained 184 yards to 17 on the ground, 17 first downs to one, and Rodgers put Cloud to shame gaining 90 yards to Jack's four. Few visitors in Kenan have forgotten one play in particular when Rodgers barreled through the line, met his adversary head on, and bowled him for additional yards.

Justice? Put down another 77 yards on the ground and 83 in the air.

Carolina fans, who had made New Orleans reservations, forgot the Sugar Bowl. It appeared out of the question—until the next Saturday.

On November 14, the Tar Heels proved they had the stuff of champions once again. This time the locale was Washington, and Jim Tatum had his Maryland club primed to upset the Tar Heels. Tatum, too, wanted to lick his friend and former coach, Snavely.

Before the Terps knew what had happened, the score was 28-7 and it was halftime. The final: 49-20.

Washington fans in Griffith Stadium went wild over Justice as a punter. One quick kick went 65 yards, and another went 83 yards, including roll, before squeaking into the end zone.

Tatum, as is his custom, ambled into the visitors' dressing room to offer his congratulations. He walked over to Justice and shook his hand warmly.

"Charlie," said the coach, "we wanted to find out if you were a man today. We're convinced. You took a lot of punishment and you came back for more. None of my Maryland boys hold any doubts about your ability to take it."

Then it was the Big One—Duke.

Justice was at his best. He gained 133 yards in 14 rushes, passed 47 yards with five for nine, averaged 45.7 yards a boot, and did everything but take home the goal posts.

A touchdown run which is still talked about in hot stove circles is the 43-yard touchdown gallop of Choo Choo against the Blue Devils.

Coach Snavely described it mildly.

"Charlie's touchdown run was one of the greatest I've ever seen," the usually reticent Gray Fox said. "When the play started, we could see that they had shifted

74

their defense to stop it. But somehow he broke through. They almost had him behind the line, but he got away."

Justice did appear trapped. He cut to his left, back to his right, reversed his field, cut back again. The blockers looked over their shoulders, not knowing what to do next.

Big Ted Hazlewood hit one Duke player and sat on him. Justice whizzed past.

"Hey, Ted," the player yelled, "lemme up. The play's over."

"Heck no," said Hazlewood, "not with that Justice. You never know when he might be coming this way again."

Undoubtedly Justice passed that way again.

After the 20-0 game was over, Snavely couldn't contain a smile as he walked off the field.

"See you at the Sugar Bowl, Coach," a fan yelled.

"Could be," he answered, a sparkle in his eye. "I've never been happier."

Meanwhile, a few yards away, Justice's teammates were carrying him off the field.

In their jubilation, Tar Heel followers were a little worried. Virginia was the final game at Charlottesville, and Virginians—William and Mary to be exact—had been hard on their team.

The fears were ungrounded. It was all Justice again. He passed for two touchdowns (31 yards to Cox, 40 to Weiner), scored two himself (one on an 80-yard gallop), and rushed for 159 yards. He also completed four of six passes for another 87 yards. The windup was by 34-12.

The Sugar Bowl bid was accepted before the steam had settled in the showers. The Tar Heels were off to glory land, and big, bad Oklahoma was ahead.

It was Christmas in Hammond, La., for the Tar Heels, and a time when a "tummyache" made headlines. For three days before the Sugar Bowl game, Charlie Justice lived on soups and other liquids.

The secret of Justice's illness was fairly well kept until the day before the game. When a reporter stumbled onto the details, the North Carolina press couldn't have been more concerned had the governor slipped into an alligator pit.

Rumors grew. One "reliable source" had Charlie just before being wheeled into the operating room for an appendectomy. Another felt sure he would miss the Oklahoma game unless an oxygen tent accompanied him on the field. The frantic reporting was reminiscent of the famed Babe Ruth illness during the mid-20's.

Meanwhile, the gay caravan which followed the Tar Heels to what was hoped would be laurels and new prestige with a good showing in the Sugar Bowl was making the most of its holiday.

Wrote Furman Bisher in *The Charlotte News*: "If the winner could be determined by whooping and hollering and ripping and roaring, it would be Carolina over the Sooners by the length of Canal Street. There can't be anybody left back in the old

home state. There are enough folks here to drown not only the Oklahomans, but the Creole natives, too. The night club entertainers have been harassed all week by shouts of 'All the Way Choo Choo.' "

The largest crowd ever to see a football game in the South turned out on January 1, 1949. The official count in Tulane Stadium read 85,000.

A hundred or more football players trotted out for pre-game warmups. One of them was Charlie Justice, complete with stomach.

The contest was a letdown from the excitement of the Georgia fray two years previous. Oklahoma built a 14-6 lead and, using the good judgment that a win would be far better than taking the chances an offensive show would entail, played a control game.

Justice, rushed hard in the first quarter when the Tar Heels were diving deep into Sooner territory, hurried a pass that was intercepted by Linebacker Myrle Greathouse of the opposition. Always opportunists, the Big Seven champs converted it into a touchdown.

Carolina came back with a score by Rodgers on a two-yard buck; then the usually glue-fingered Weiner dropped a Justice pass in the end zone for what could have been the go-ahead marker.

The half ended at 7-6, Oklahoma.

Bud Wilkinson's Sooners picked up a second half score, then stressed possession with a grinding game. Jack Mitchell called the plays from his quarterback post and kept the situation well in hand. For his generalship, he was voted the outstanding player in the game.

There were many writers, however, who tapped Justice for the role of MVP. He had pulled off runs of nine, 10, 13, 25, 11, 14 and eight yards. He kicked four times—for 65, 65, 57 and 53 yards, a superlative exhibition. He recovered a fumble. And his pass that might have changed the complexion of the game was muffed.

The plucky, never-say-die Choo Choo took the defeat hard. He ran to the dressing room, pulled a blanket over his head, and stayed hidden for ten minutes, a dismal figure in a gloomy alcove.

"I lost it—you can say that," he told sportswriters.

"I don't see how the kid went as far as he did in his condition," said an admiring, saddened Snavely.

An hour later, when Charlie had showered and dressed, he was amazed to find several hundred youngsters still standing outside the stadium seeking his autograph. He signed, but without much enthusiasm for the task.

"They must think this is the Oklahoma side," he tried to quip.

Things were happier that night at Antoine's celebrated restaurant.

Wilkinson, free with his praise, commented: "I've never seen a single wing team do more with a ball than Carolina. There's no question about Justice being a great back. He was the player we feared the most and he showed it."

There was a reason for frowns at the Sugar Bowl

Sid Varney, the stubby guard, brought a note of humor into the Carolina showcase. Varney, heaping his plate with the superb dishes prepared for the athletes, recalled an incident on the field with Buddy Burris, the All-American guard for the Sooners.

"He was giving me a rough time all day," said Sid. "I finally told him, 'Burris, I know I'm good—but do you have to hold me on EVERY play?'"

The behemoth Highsmith noted that Burris had broken a bone in his hand during the game. Chan pointed to a black eye he was wearing and vowed it was the cause of the Burris injury.

"Why didn't you hit him back?" demanded Varney.

"Sir," said Chan, utilizing a squeaky falsetto, "that would not have been the sporting thing to do."

IX

END OF AN ERA

Some days they could do no wrong.

And some days they did little that was right.

It was that kind of year. A time for laughing, a time for praying, a time for wishing.

As the days grew shorter and December came rushing like an oncoming tide, it was a time, too, for nostalgia.

It was a time to listen as the Tower chimes played "Hark the Sound," to stop and savor the crispness of the autumn air, when the sandy paths around Kenan Stadium were highways to glory, and when the girl on your arm was just a little prettier than last week or the week before.

Something wonderful was fast approaching its final chapter—and you clung to it like a tot clutching a favorite ragdoll.

＊　　　＊　　　＊

SEPTEMBER of 1949 brought renewed enthusiasm for football at Chapel Hill— but there was not the ability to go with the spirit. Gone were many of the stalwarts up front and gone were Rodgers, Pupa and others. Only a shadow of the great teams of the past three years remained.

Football historians may look upon the season in many ways:

As one in which the Tar Heels made their third bowl trip in four years.

The year Notre Dame was given a scare by a Justice-less Tar Heel team.

The year of a truly fabulous Duke victory—the fourth of the Justice reign.

The year Choo Choo Justice wound up a brilliant collegiate career.

N. C. State was a stout team, as always, but its prowess brought it few laurels. The Tar Heels opened with a 26 to 6 win over the Wolfpack. Justice accounted for two of the four touchdowns, and 44,000 fans said the Tar Heels "had it again."

"It was just too much Weiner and Justice," Beattie Feathers said later. "The most satisfying part of the game to me is the fact I won't have to see them again."

Justice scored one on a 39-yard burst and passed to Kenny Powell for another. Weiner was everywhere—starting the season on his way to a national collegiate pass reception record of 52.

There were flashes of brilliance. The Tar Heels had it—but only in spots.

Georgia followed at Chapel Hill. It was 21-14, a hard-pressed win. Justice hit Weiner for a touchdown pass, scored one himself and was the workhorse. It was evident the Choo Choo could make or break the 1949 season. He was to get limited help from eager but less talented young Tar Heels.

At the end of the half it was only 7-0, Carolina. Justice went to work. As an example of his determined spirit and physical ability, here's a blueprint of his activity:

Billy Hayes took the second half kickoff on the three and returned to the 16.

Justice carried once.

Hayes carried again.

Justice to Powell, eight yards; Justice to Weiner, 30 yards; Justice in the line once, twice, three times; Justice to Fred Sherman, six yards; Justice to Weiner five yards; Hayes up the middle, 13 yards; Justice for the TD. Georgia didn't recover.

Football coaches, fans, players around the Conference wanted to "get the Tar Heels." The handwriting was on the field. Carolina could be taken on a "right" Saturday. Who would do it?

A strong South Carolina team tried. A tense crowd of 28,500 gathered at Columbia to watch. It was the largest paid football attendance in the state's history.

Charlie held the fort again with good help from Sherman and Hayes.

Charlie ran, passed to Art for eight completions, kicked—and South Carolina fell by a 28-13 margin.

Maybe it wouldn't be done. All eyes were on Chapel Hill again. Had Snavely moulded another power out of a bunch of newcomers and his old pros — Justice, Weiner and Powell?

It looked that way on October 15 when the Choo Choo chugged for three of four touchdowns in the 28-14 win over stubborn Wake Forest. The skeptical were

81

Notre Dame, 1949, his saddest day

temporarily silenced. Justice ran for three scores, picked up 102 yards and Carolina jumped to sixth in the *Associated Press* poll.

Celebrations from Alderman Dormitory to the back booth of Jeff's were short-lived.

A headline told the story the next Sunday: LSU SHOCKS WORLD BY UPSETTING CAROLINA, 13-7.

Perhaps the world wasn't shocked, but Louisiana State had not been figured as the team to deal the Tar Heels their first defeat since early 1947 (except for two Sugar Bowl games) and its first loss in 22 regular season games.

The *Associated Press* reported on Justice: "While Choo Choo Charlie was far from up to tops, he still remained a thorn in the side of the Bengals. He roamed the field like a caged beast and, except for desperate tackles, would have fled for tallies on several occasions. The danger signal was up when he had the ball, and his light punts, averaging 47.5 yards, kept the surging Tigers at bay most of the time."

It was a major upset, no doubt about it, and one shrouded in controversy. The game was played at night, a warm, dry evening, in Baton Rouge and Tar Heel fans howled that LSU had watered the field in an effort to stop the quick-cutting Justice. The charges were denied, although it was admitted that the field could have been sprinkled the afternoon of the contest. The battle of words raged, but the defeat stood in the record books.

Snavely admitted, "They gave us a good trimming. Don't be misled into believing that a wet field or other factors caused us to get beat."

The licked Tar Heels returned home the next week, but business got no better. It crashed. Tennessee, led by Hal Littleford, Hank Lauricello and Herky Payne, did the wrecking. The score: 35 to 6 in favor of Tennessee.

It was the first Tar Heel loss in Kenan since the Wake Forest game in 1947, and it hung heavy in the minds of the loyal. Was this the end? It appeared so. Sighed Justice, limping and bruised: "That was the worst physical beating I've ever taken."

Snavely tried to rally the team.

"Men," he told them Monday, "we're starting a new season right now."

The "new" season saw William and Mary fall by a 20-14 score, respectable enough in rugged Southern Conference play, but it took final period action.

It was a nifty 75-yard Justice punt return that turned the trick with just three minutes left.

The win was costly. Justice sprained an ankle. And Notre Dame, the King of Big Time Football, was next. This one was scheduled for New York's Yankee Stadium.

Despite the two losses and the closeness of the Indian game, the Tar Heel student body forgot its classwork and opened an "On-To-New York" crusade.

83

A toss of the coin at the Cotton Bowl game

Cars moved northward bumper to bumper, gaily decorated with Confederate flags, blue-and-white bunting and sweatered coeds. A "Stop Sitko" chant could be heard at every stoplight. The Sitko tirade was aimed at Grantland Rice, the great sportswriter who had picked the Notre Dame halfback, Emil Sitko, over Choo Choo on his All-American team. Now the Tar Heels wanted to show Granny. It was a carnival the night before the game. College kids invaded Times Square and traffic stopped. A pep rally was held at the intersection of Broadway and 42nd Street.

Growled a New York cop, shaking his head in disgust: "Trying to preserve order here is like fighting a locust invasion with a water pistol."

Unfortunately, a Justice-Sitko duel didn't materialize. Justice was seriously ailing this time, appeared in the game only twice—once to hold the ball on an unsuccessful placement attempt; the other time he rushed onto the field to challenge a referee's decision.

Dick Bunting, a slight kid from Roanoke, Virginia, spelled Justice against Notre Dame and did a tremendous job, before 67,000 fans, half of whom were Southerners. The Tar Heels led by 6-0 in the first period; it was 6-6 at the half; and 15-6 after the third. The fourth quarter saw the Irish pour on 27 points. Some of the blocks would have smashed tanks.

The disputed play worried the Tar Heel fans. They booed and hissed what they called an illegal forward-lateral (shades of New Year's '47) from Bobby Williams to Leon Hart to Billy Barrett. But it did give them a chance to see a dejected Justice on the field again—arguing with an official.

The final was 42-6 and one couldn't find the Tar Heels in the standings with a microscope.

The first half stand against Notre Dame was regarded as something of a moral victory for Carolina. The press of the nation noted it in column after column of vivid adjectives, but the Tar Heels would get no respite from work. Duke was next.

What followed was one of the most frantic finishes in UNC history. The 21-20 win is etched indelibly in the memory of the fans.

It was a game in which officials ruled that one play remained after the gun sounded and Mike Souchak, now a leading pro golfer, tried a desperate 20-yard field goal for the Blue Devils after "regulation" play was over. Art Weiner, untouched, rushed in to block it.

Before that, Tar Heel fans crowded onto the playing field. They reached for the spectacular Justice, but he fought them off. He ran anxiously along the sidelines pleading, "Please, please stand back!"

They stood back—and watched Weiner as he smashed the attempt. Then they broke out.

It was a Justice day again, that frigid afternoon in Duke Stadium. Charlie won a mountain of praise and dazzled 57,500 fans with his play.

Afterwards, some asked Snavely if Justice was "the best you've ever coached."

"Well, he played on one leg today, and he was just about the best I've ever seen. Under the circumstances, he was the greatest. I never thought he would last through the first period."

After four and a half minutes in that opening quarter, Tar Heel hopes were at low ebb. Billy Cox scampered 75 yards for a touchdown and Justice was carried off the field for the fourth time in his career. It was the ankle again. Novocain came in handy and he returned to action.

Returned? He busted out! He took a pass from Hayes to score one touchdown and passed to Weiner for two more. The final toss was a spectacular 45-yarder.

The Tar Heels scored three times—Justice had a hand in all three. He added a 68-yard quick-kick at one crucial point which rolled dead on the Duke one.

Veteran Wallace Wade, who had been beaten by Justice and the Tar Heels four times in a row, was not disappointed in his team. The defeat hurt, but he didn't take any luster from the Tar Heel win.

"From the standpoint of ability," he said, "this was the finest game a Duke team has ever played. Yes, the finest."

Justice often had a houseful of relatives on football weekends and he would spend his Saturday nights at the Carolina Inn. He shunned the parties that raged loud and long into the night and soothed his sore muscles with sleep.

Sunday mornings were always a treat. There would be coffee in bed, the papers to read and a restful few hours before the handshakes of the well-meaning alumni.

That morning the columnists had been particularly kind, embarrassingly flattering. Charlie was turning from paper to paper when he heard a chant from below. Walking up the street beneath his window at the Inn were some students who hadn't quit celebrating. They were singing, "All the Way Choo Choo," at the top of their lungs.

A half-smile on his face, Justice hopped out of bed, raised the window, and, hiding himself just out of view, yelled, "Why don't you guys forget about that fellow and let us get some sleep up here?"

Little did the angry mob below realize the unprintable answer they returned was directed at their idol, but one who didn't take himself too seriously.

UNC stock shot upward again. There was bowl talk in the air. This time it was Cotton, not Sugar. Dallas looked like a fine place to spend New Year's. The Tar Heels went there after the final game—the 14-7 win over Virginia.

A limping, jerky-running Justice scored his last Kenan Stadium touchdown against the Cavaliers. Game and talented to the end, he was a crippled player in that finale—but he didn't let his fans down. Charlie scored, passed to the elusive Art for a touchdown and a great career appeared all but finished.

The Virginia team, which would have received the Cotton Bowl bid had it won the game, was crestfallen. Coach Guepe commented: "Disappointed? I'll say I'm disappointed, but that's a part of this game. Those same guys lick us year after year.

tice was the first to admit it took ten other teammates to make a play click.

The only way to handle Justice is to lasso him and keep him tied to the bench."

On Monday, January 2, 1950, some 76,000 fans pushed into the Cotton Bowl to watch the Rice Owls of Jess Neely manhandle the Tar Heels, 27-13.

It was 27-0 until the last quarter of the game and in characteristic fashion, Justice passed to Paul Rizzo for one touchdown, lateraled to him for another.

One embarrassed North Carolina reporter wrote: "A University of North Carolina football team whose best friends doubted that it belonged in a bowl game this year has successfully defended that opinion. There is no question about how it happened. They were thoroughly, humiliatingly and discouragingly hammered down by a fine Rice team.

"Charlie Justice, who wheeled into the roundhouse after a long and illustrious run, was not himself, even if his 62 yards rushing and 62 yards passing appear respectable. The gallant Choo Choo reminded me of a tired, aged pitcher with a sore arm, giving it everything he had to last out the stretch and win with guts and nerve, if nothing else."

But the Choo Choo didn't go into retirement.

The next Saturday he was at Jacksonville, Florida, to captain the Southerners against the North in the first Senior Bowl game. His chief rival and good friend, SMU's Doak Walker, was leader of the "Yankees."

A spectator at practice asked Charlie if he thought his team could win against the abundance of stars in the opposite lineup.

"I'll put it this way," said Justice. "The game is based on the winner getting 60 per cent of the net receipts and the losers getting 40 per cent. We wouldn't be down here if we figured to take home only 40."

Coached by Stout Steve Owen, then of the New York Giants, it was a 22-13 victory for Justice and Company. Among the brilliant stars of the show were Wake Forest's Red O'Quinn, Weiner and Powell of UNC, Auburn's Travis Tidwell, who won the Most Valuable trophy as a quarterback, and others.

Eddie LeBaron of College of the Pacific, later Justice's teammate with the Redskins, quarterbacked the North, coached by the late Bo McMillin of the Detroit Lions.

Weiner, voted the game's top lineman, hauled in eight catches for 143 yards. Justice, playing the "T" formation after four years of single wing, didn't see the ball as often as his UNC tailback spot allowed. Early in the game, Owen grabbed him and said: "Charlie, we want to win and that LeBaron will kill us with his passes. Play some defense for me, will you?"

Justice nodded. Victory was the thing.

Charlie starred, nonetheless. He threw a running pass to Weiner for 15 yards, carried twice for gains of seven and 10 yards and first downs each try. He averaged 53 yards on three kicks and hauled back punts of 26 and 37 yards from safety.

Commented Owen: "What a boy—that Justice. He won for us with that great

89

ach Snavely at his favorite pastime with
nny Powell, Doak Walker and Charlie

runback on LeBaron's punt in the fourth quarter. It led to our third touchdown and it meant the game."

After the Senior Bowl, Charlie said he was through.

Well, that's what he said.

X

THE ALL-STARS' NO. 1 BOY

The long hard season was over. The ever-optimistic Tar Heel fandom looked hopefully to "next year," but you sensed a kind of finality on the campus, a goodbye to glory in every conversation.

Raymond Hutchins, the tireless groundskeeper at Chapel Hill, put Kenan's properties away with loving care.

The yard markers, the tarpaulin and the water sprinklers were hauled to the long, low steel buildings behind the field house.

The Stadium was tucked away like Sleeping Beauty—and a hush fell over Chapel Hill.

For Charlie Justice it appeared to be a sentimental goodbye to football.

*   *   *

HIS COLLEGIATE career at an end, Charlie Justice suddenly found himself deluged with offers—and advice. The professional game wanted him, business firms presented attractive opportunities, manufacturers sought endorsements, coaches invited him to join their staffs—and the University had a suggestion, too. The University was headquarters for the new Medical Foundation of North Carolina, Inc., whose function was to raise funds on behalf of the University Medical School. It was sug-

gested that Justice would make an ideal public relations man for the Foundation, going about the state preaching good health and medical facilities.

Charlie listened carefully to all propositions and to every opinion. He wanted to please everybody, although that was patently impossible. What to do? In the end, it was the University's suggestion that held the answer. His loyalty to the University was immense; he remembered that a brother might have lived had adequate medical care been available during his childhood; he even once fleetingly thought of becoming a doctor. So, instead of accepting glossier offers, he decided to go with the Foundation. He was going to pay back a debt to his university and to his state, he said. It was so-long to football. He turned down even an invitation to the College All-Star game.

But Justice later became unhappy in Chapel Hill with the Foundation. The idea was a good one, he said, but he was no orator and no smooth public relations type. He would stick to his commitment, but play one last game of football.

On the spur of the moment he called Chicago sportswriter Arch Ward, the founder and guiding light behind the College All-Star game.

"I'd sure like to play in the game," he said.

Ward hesitated. His group selected the outstanding college players of the previous year and they played a game against the National Football League champions. The squad was limited to 50 players and the agreement between Ward and the professionals stated that only four players who had agreed to play with a pro club might participate in the All-Star game. The number was limited because the professionals feared their investments—the draft choices—would be injured. Charlie knew he was in the clear because, although Washington had his draft rights, he would not be playing for them.

Under the rules of professional football, each team in the NFL "drafts" the collegiate players of the previous season. The players have no choice or control over their professional destinies. The teams can trade the player, sell him outright or release him. Justice was the No. 1 draft choice of the Washington Redskins and, although there was no indication he would ever play for the Redskins, they held onto his rights like a swimmer to his life belt.

"We've got four Redskins, Charlie," Ward said. "Are you sure you're not turning pro?"

"I have given my word to the Medical Foundation," he answered.

"Well, I have my 50 men, but if you want to take a chance and be number 51, come on out."

Charlie took the next flight to Chicago, but his reception by the staff was less than enthusiastic. He hung around and practiced a little, but was selected only for the kickoff receiving team under the platoon system.

Charlie and his two All-Star buddies, Doak Walker of Southern Methodist and Eddie LeBaron of the College of the Pacific, made the most of the trip to the Stars' Delafield, Wisconsin, training camp.

93

pair of All-Americans, Justice and his pal from SMU, Doak Walker

The three "country boys" had a ball in their own, quiet sort of way. They were watermelon lovers and the first day in camp staked out a small country store which carried the commodity.

"Put one on ice every afternoon," Charlie told the proprietor, "and we'll come by and pick it up."

Every afternoon after practice the trio walked to the store, purchased their chilled melon, took it outside and sat on the curb munching large slices.

Charlie's old friend and college blocking back, Joe Wright, his wife, and Sarah journeyed to Chicago a few days later to watch Charlie play.

"I sure am sorry you all came," he said. "If you miss the opening kickoff you might not see me."

They were late for the opening kickoff, but they didn't miss Choo Choo in action.

Justice, with little LeBaron, a half-pint from the West Coast, trotted onto Soldier Field to comprise a half of the receiving team's backfield. After receiving, they were instructed to run the first series of plays to determine the Philadelphia Eagles' defense.

They moved the ball well. So well, in fact, that Dr. Eddie Anderson of Iowa, the Stars' coach, told LeBaron and Justice to stay in the lineup for a while. It came as a bit of a surprise to the Steve Van Buren-led Eagles who had read glowing notices on practically everyone but these two.

And did they play! LeBaron was a picture of perfection as a passer and ball handler.

Of Charlie, Francis J. Powers of the *Chicago Daily News* wrote, "Justice was all the runner his Dixie admirers claimed."

Early that evening, before the Wrights and Sarah had settled in their seats, the duo had 88,885 cheering fans on their side.

The Mighty Mites were on their way to a wrecking job.

Eddie handed off to Charlie and most of the experienced Eagles were suckered by a great fake by Ohio State's Curley Morrison. Justice continued on his way, heading for the east sideline and cantered 31 yards to the Eagles' 23. For good measure he chipped in with another 12-yard sparkler that put the Eagles' backs to the wall. They knew not what to make of Justice and while they tried to figure him out, LeBaron gave to Ralph Pasquariello of Villanova who bucked it over.

Oddly enough, Justice might have scored the first touchdown which went to the bullish Pasquariello. The goal posts in the All-Star game were set by professional rules on the goal line, not the back line of the end zone as in college play. Charlie thought he had scored—when he was slammed to the ground.

Not only did the Choo Choo set up that first touchdown, but he also scored the second and set up the third score, a field goal.

he Justices as spectators—with ex-coach Crowell Little

In the second period LeBaron found himself trapped behind the line while trying to pass. He was on the Eagles' 40. Charlie was downfield praying for Eddie to find him.

LeBaron ran around like a scared rabbit, and two towering Eagles made stabs for him. The crowd groaned, for it seemed certain he would be massacred. But finally he saw Charlie—and cut loose.

Charlie lunged for the ball, found the handle, and ran for his life. He didn't stop until he was over the goal. The play covered 60 yards and Justice never ran better than those last 35.

Choo Choo contributed another long run, one of 47 yards, but his twisting 28-yarder later set up a field goal by Gorden Soltau which put the game on ice, 17-7, for the upstart collegians. When the final figures were totaled, Powers wrote, "He lugged the ball nine times for 133 yards or 48 more than the Eagles could register. LeBaron and Justice, they were a pair."

Wilfrid Smith of the *Tribune* added, "Justice's running was exceptional. No halfback has done better against the pro champions."

The next day as Justice sat in a Chicago hotel room, the telephone rang.

"Now do you think you're too small for pro ball?" said the caller.

Charlie blinked. It was George Marshall, owner of the Redskins, calling.

"Charlie," he added, "I'm sending you a blank check. Fill it in."

"I'm sorry, Mr. Marshall, but I promised the people at Chapel Hill . . ."

The Choo Choo heard another voice that day. A radio announcer told of the selection by the sportswriters of the All-Star game's Most Valuable Player. His name: Charlie Justice. *"Charlie Justice, 1950"* was added to a list which included such names as Cecil Isbell of Purdue, Glenn Dobbs of Tulsa, Pat Harder of Wisconsin, Charley Trippi of Georgia, Buddy Young of Illinois and Elroy Hirsch of Wisconsin.

In September of 1950, a hot, muggy September in Chapel Hill, Charlie was seated behind a desk wondering what to do next. Chapel Hillians, who walked down tree-shaded Pittsboro Street, could see the figure through open windows in an old barracks structure. He read magazines, drummed his fingers on the desk top, scribbled doodles and, like all players, scratched a few football diagrams—plays designed, absolutely, to go all-the-way.

He was billed as an employee of the Medical Foundation, but he felt much like a cheerleader who is suddenly told to go in as a left halfback.

It didn't last long.

Before the pro season was over, Charlie was in uniform for the Redskins.

One of his greatest moments—receiving the MV trophy from the College All-Star game of 195

XI

JUSTICE FOR THE REDSKINS

Just one season—and there are many changes.

No longer is there wild exuberance in dressing rooms, or scenic pine-lined paths to the arena, or halftime high school bands.

This is the Big Time now—the pros.

Big Time where they sing "Hail to the Redskins," not "Hark the Sound"; where linemen are giants—all of them, and where you pick up your check on Monday.

*   *   *

"THE ONLY things wrong with Charlie Justice's professional football career were that he didn't come into the National Football League soon enough—nor did he stay long enough."

George Preston Marshall, a large man with unlimited ideas and an eye on money bags, made the cold appraisal of Charlie Justice. Marshall looks over an athlete much like Elizabeth Arden would look over a colt at the Maine Chance stables: Will he produce? Can he develop? How strong is he? How durable? How fast is he? Will he be good as a two-year-old or a three-year-old?

Marshall's money is in the Washington, D. C., football team. It is a business, a big business. His job is to produce crowds, and to draw customers he needs two vital ingredients: an attraction in a big name player and a winning team.

99

edskins Marshall and Coach Herman Ball make a chief out of Justice

If he could get Charlie Justice, Marshall would be the envy of the NFL, for he would have a chance to hit the right combination with a rookie. When Justice's four years were up at Carolina, he had added further prestige to an already outstanding career as the bright star of the Senior Bowl game, and the Most Valuable Player in the famed College All-Star game.

Marshall rubbed his hands with glee. Mention the name Justice around Washington and folks got excited. North Carolina and Virginia were within cheering distance of Griffith Stadium, and these states were where Justice was championed. Marshall could picture the famed Redskins' marching band playing Hank Beebe's and Orville Campbell's song, "All the Way Choo Choo" and a mental picture of a packed stadium flashed across his mind.

There was only one hitch: No Justice.

Marshall had tried, but Justice's steadfast refusal to give up his promise to the University resisted all luring offers of money.

But Charlie was not long for the Medical Foundation. It was like making a plow horse out of Man o' War. It just didn't make sense. He belonged somewhere in football—as an official, player, coach, trainer, anything.

Then Snavely called. He wanted Charlie to join his staff for the 1950 season. Charlie was ready. He told the Foundation people that he was not happy and that he couldn't earn his salary. They agreed to let him out of his commitment and he was ready to join his old coach.

Campus politics entered the picture. There was talk that it wouldn't be right for Justice to switch from on campus job to another. It smacked, said some of the oldtimers, of campus raiding. No matter how far-fetched it sounded to the innocent Justice, it was decided that he would join Snavely after the first of January, 1951.

Marshall came into the picture again. He still wanted his No. 1 draft choice, for the Redskins needed running strength. Charlie at last said yes. Although he was out of shape and had not worked since the All-Star contest, he reported to Washington and active football.

Tar Heel fans were jubilant. Justice was going to play again. They had not, however, calculated the odds against any measure of stardom. He has missed the valuable exhibition games and five regular season games. It was mid-October when he moved into an apartment in Washington and began studying a massive book of Redskin plays. Not only was he faced with learning a new offense, but he would be running from the T-formation instead of the single wing. He had not played the "T" since his Bainbridge days.

But Marshall had confidence in him. He offered $1,000 per game—and it was good professional money. For Marshall, it was repaid in full by the tremendous crowds he drew that first season.

The overweight, short-winded Choo Choo reported with a feeling an anxiety. He had never been sure about pro football.

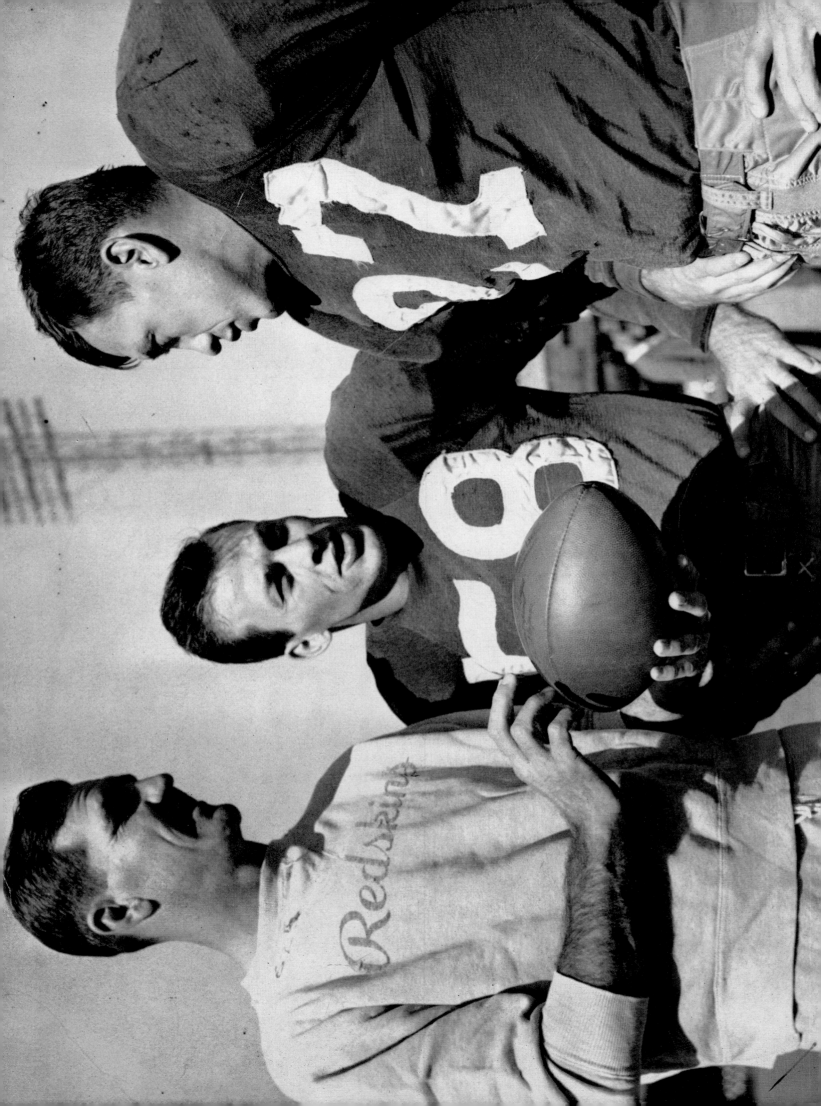

"I wasn't keen on the game," he confided to a friend at the time. "I had figured I was too small, and I had a mental block against it."

The Redskins had Justice's NFL draft rights, but that didn't stop others from asking. The Charlotte Clippers had offered him a deal and Keith Molesworth's Richmond Rebels, a smart-looking club, offered a reported $30,000 for his services. Ottawa of the Canadian pro league made a pitch.

That first year, 1950, Charlie played in the five games remaining on the schedule. Playing just half the season, he still outgained all the squad's other backs in those games and ended the season as the club's second leading rusher.

He was an amazing athlete to watch in the pros, for the 'Skins slanted him off tackle and there, in the murderous junction of the lines, he met the most feared players in football. He met them, often, but after he averaged a lofty 5.4 yards a carry.

Washington was happy with Charlie, and Marshall gave him a $1,000 bonus to show his pleasure. The Choo Choo was still not convinced that he was a professional. He had done all that anyone had dreamed he would do, but Justice wanted to go back home.

He returned to Chapel Hill and joined Snavely's staff. He was a good recruiter, a good scout, and a promising young coach. He was as watched on Navy Field as any of the athletes, and it appeared to the more imaginative, angle-seeking sportswriters that Justice would be charged with developing his own successor.

It was nothing more than a romantic and interesting notion, for, while he saw many stellar young high school tailbacks report for duty, there was no Justice in the lot.

Marshall still had an idea that Charlie could be lured to Washington—and he was correct. The money was good in comparison to the salary of an assistant football coach.

A story hit the headlines that Justice had signed a three-year pact for $50,000. It was false. Actually, he signed for $12,000 for the 1952 season and received $10,000 a year for the 1953 and 1954 seasons. It was just another in a series of exaggerated stories about the great wealth of the young man.

Marshall was indignant at the rumors.

"That guy has been maligned as much as any athlete I know. I know it just isn't true that he received all those favors—financial and otherwise, from the University of North Carolina."

Justice was back in uniform—and the slow process of getting in shape started painfully in a West Coast training camp.

Stories leaked back to the East that Justice was looking sharp. He appeared to be getting better and better. The timing of old was clicking and the Choo Choo was rolling.

On the night of August 21, 1952, the Redskins faced the Los Angeles Rams and before the dew had settled on the Coliseum turf, Justice's name was bannered in

103

headlines from coast-to-coast. He turned in one of the finest one-man shows in professional football history before 87,582 fans.

He ran like a cat with a tin-can tied to his tail; he was the fox with the hounds comin' up fast. He darted, turned, twisted, scooted to the tune of shouts and cheers of the thousands who watched.

He piled up 199 yards in 11 carries, and, if fate had not stepped in again, would have broken all pro records. He had runs of 49, 53 and 63 yards, all starting deep in his own territory.

A freak accident occurred in the closing quarter and the Choo Choo broke his wrist. It was a jolting climax.

The West Coast, which worships the bizarre and incredulous, was enraptured by the feat of Justice. He became its personal hero overnight — although his wrist was encased in a cast he would wear for six weeks.

Former Carolina cheerleader Kay Kyser, once a zany bandleader, was visiting in Hollywood at the time of Justice's explosive performance.

"I was just another actor trying to make a million," quipped Kay. "When the big shots learned I was a personal friend of Charlie's, I immediately found doors opening. My popularity zoomed and I suddenly found what it meant to be a celebrity."

Marshall and the coaching staff weren't so gay. The one-night stand had been costly for the team and the box office.

"Too bad," commented Marshall. "Charlie was headed for his greatest year in the National League. There's no telling how far he could have gone in top physical shape."

Four games later and a few pounds heavier, Choo Choo returned to duty with the 'Skins. Although he had missed three regular season contests and one exhibition, he broke into the lineup and was off flying.

Leon Heath ultimately was the Redskins' top runner, piling up a lead in yardage by playing the full schedule. Charlie was in second place with a 4.8 yards per carry mark and the Redskins were crying, "Wait 'til next year."

The year 1953 rolled around and there was no indication that Charlie, although no longer a light-footed kid, was slowing down. The Redskins had been losing. (Not since 1948 had Washington won more than four regular season games and the pressure was on.) Justice was needed—for a full season. Was this to be the year? Fans held their breath during the training season. Thus far the Choo Choo had only played a part of two seasons, and they wondered what the guy could do as a full-timer.

Charlie came through. There were no runs of great distances—nor were there many in the entire league, for the pros defense too strongly—but he whacked off the yardage with remarkable regularity. His 616 yards for a 5.4 average topped the Redskins and was superior to his rushing net at Carolina in both 1947 and 1948. What

105

was even more important to the cheering Washington fans was the Eastern Division rushing title which came to Justice at the end of the year.

There were great individual games, too, as Justice spread his elusive running evenly among the league's best clubs. He ran 114 yards against the Chicago Cardinals one Sunday and laughed at their new defenses in the next meeting, scooting for 127 that time. The New York Giants watched him dash past them for 114 yards in another game and arch-rival Baltimore "held" him to 115 yards.

It was a great year and the Redskins settled down to what looked like long-term prosperity.

During the off-season, Charlie made numerous talks and visits to schools and hospitals. At the Poinsett Hotel in Greenville, S. C., he checked in one evening and decided on a shoe-shine before departing for his engagement.

The elderly colored attendant worked hard and willingly. The shoe leather glittered. Charlie rewarded him with a fifty-cent piece.

"Nice fellow," said the shine to his next customer.

"Not only nice," volunteered the customer, "but he's a celebrity."

"I likes to know celebrities," he said. "Which one is he?"

"Why," boasted the Justice admirer, "he's just the most famous and best football player ever to come out the Carolinas."

"Lordy," sighed the attendant, "don't try to tell me that's J. C. Caroline?"

The 1954 season found Charlie running hard again. It was a disappointing, weaker Redskin team that year, but the energetic little halfback kept up his steady pace. Halfback Billy Wells led in yardage gained, but Justice was second.

The 'Skins won only three games, but it could have been worse had not the versatile Justice helped out by punting. This was a new duty for Justice in the pros where the league has many specialists. But he was not put to shame—not with a 40.3-yard average. He wound up eighth in the league in that department.

Marshall, who had seen Charlie live up to his hopes as a runner, a good punter and pass receiver (plus some action on the defensive unit), offered another $10,000 contract. Already Charlie was the 'Skins third longest gainer in history in a group which had such aces as Cliff Battle, Dick Todd and others. His professional records stood at a steady four-yards plus every time he touched the ball.

Marshall talked long and earnestly. He reflected upon the decision later.

"Charlie was one of the best runners in modern football. It is too bad he didn't play the T all his career. He would have been a great pass catcher in addition to his proven talent as a runner. Charlie was a fine kicker and, strange to say, because of his size, an excellent blocker."

Marshall was not the first to mention the T, but he often strengthened his argument by going back to Charlie's Bainbridge days—and he had seen Justice then, too.

107

Charlie found a friend in a former Wake Forest foe, Harry Dowda

"It was proved at Bainbridge that he was a natural for the T formation. He was just a baby, but he ran against the older men, the professionals, and look what he did."

Marshall, adjudged one of the keenest promoters in football, tried to get Justice to stay in the pro game, but he was unsuccessful.

"Thanks," Charlie told him, "but it is time for an old man to hang up his cleats." And so he did at the conclusion of the 1954 season.

XII

MONEY AND MYTHS

When Charlie Justice, after his brief "retirement" from active football, decided to join the Washington Redskins in the fall of 1950, wags made the most of it. A standard bromide of the time was, "It's a shame the Choo Choo had to switch from college to the pros—and take a cut in salary."

*   *   *   *   *   *

WAS BIG MONEY involved in Justice's choice of North Carolina over the countless other colleges which also invited him to four years "on the house?"

Cynics insisted an athlete of Justice's caliber would be foolish not to put himself on the block—and sell to the highest bidder. "Next to Justice," winked the smart boys, "Snavely is the highest paid person on the football field."

Charlie heard an abundance of such talk and at times he became exasperated by smoothies who claimed they had inside information on his "scholarship."

"I won't argue with you," he'd say with a smile, "but please don't tell the income tax folks. You'll get me in a lot of trouble, because I haven't paid them a cent."

Charlie attended the University under the GI Bill of Rights. The athletic grant he normally would have received was accepted by his pretty young wife, Sarah.

There is no doubt the Justice name could have sold for a premium. Charlie admits he received offers before he entered the University, some that were staggeringly profitable and difficult for a young man just out of service to refuse.

One school brazenly suggested a bank book with a $10,000 balance. All he had to do was enroll and begin writing checks. Another, a small college with hopes of becoming a giant overnight, made him a business proposition. Play for us, enticed the agent, and there will be a percentage of the gate receipts set aside each Saturday.

Temptation was great, especially for a youngster who had grown up without luxuries and had not only himself, but a wife to support.

"I have a hard time convincing people," said Charlie time and again, "but my only arrangement with the University is a straight scholarship. There are a couple of things which shouldn't be overlooked.

"I want an education and so does my wife. We can get it at Chapel Hill. I'm not asking the school for anything more than other members of the squad. As for bartering, I hardly knew Coach Snavely when I decided to attend Carolina. The most he ever gave me was a dish of homemade ice cream."

Justice stuck with his story and no one ever disproved it.

One morning, as some of the players spent an idle hour in Y court, the center of activity on the campus during class breaks, Justice took a seat near Chan Highsmith, the lineman from Brunswick, Georgia, and George Sparger, an end, center, and sometimes blocking back, from Mount Airy, N. C.

"Say," said Chan, one of the team's practical jokers, speaking to Sparger in abnormally loud tones, "isn't that the fellow sitting over there who's making all the money?"

"You're right," asserted Sparger in mock indignation.

"Well," continued Chan, "if he's so good, maybe he won't need any of us poor boys to block for him today. Now I'm not in too much a mood for blocking anyway, are you?"

"Hate that part of the game," said Sparger.

Charlie smiled. So did the friends grouped around him.

During practice that afternoon, Coach Snavely called for a dummy scrimmage, players simply going through the motions of blocks and play patterns.

Suddenly Snavely ordered: "All right, now try it for real."

Highsmith, playing a tackle, had his mind elsewhere. He didn't hear the instructions and assumed the dummy drill was still in progress. When the ball was snapped, he was shocked to see End Joe Romano come roaring past, charge into Justice and flatten the tailback almost before he got the ball.

Charlie looked up, visibly shaken. Had Chan meant what he inferred earlier that day?

"What are you trying to do, Highsmith?" asked Charlie meekly. "Bankrupt me before we play a game?"

Big Chan grinned. The next play was identical. The 230-pounder screened Romano and Justice skipped past on a run that went the distance of the field.

Charlie, the great Otto Graham and Hollywood friend

Later, Highsmith took Charlie aside and apologized for his mental blackout.

"If you can run like you did on the last play," he told Charlie, "maybe you're worth a little bit more than the rest of us."

While there were tales of plush living, jars of hidden gold and new convertibles for each day of the week for the halfback, the Justices, Charlie and Sarah, lived a fairly modest life. They took an apartment on busy Franklin Street and this was probably the most obvious key to Charlie's importance. Housing for couples was critical at that time. The Justices were celebrities, indeed, to rate a choice spot so quickly.

"We're lucky to get it," Charlie would admit, "but it isn't exactly the swank penthouse some of the writers call it." It was an efficiency model—one room. The bed had to be made before the Justices could eat breakfast. It folded into the wall.

Later, Charlie and Sarah moved to a modest bungalow on Airport Road. So famed did the halfback become the street was renamed "Justice Drive." A neighbor was Art Weiner, the other twin in touchdown production.

Art, never without a quip, might have been responsible for some of Charlie's legendary wealth.

"I'm a man of meager needs," Art told listeners during bull sessions. "I have a stick in my kitchen with a nail in it. When they bring up the armored truck to pay off Charlie each month, I pray for a big wind. Any bills that blow into the yard, I spear. I've put myself through college that way."

Billy Carmichael Jr., comptroller of the University and one of the sharper wits of the official family, once appeared before a group to make a talk, followed by a question and answer session.

"I understand," spoke up a wiseacre in the audience, "that when Charlie Justice graduates at Carolina, there's a move to make him university president?"

The set-up was too good for Carmichael to pass.

"No, sir," he said without a trace of a smile. "We wouldn't dare subject Sarah and her child to the limited salary of a mere college president."

It sometimes reached comic proportions. A Roanoke, Virginia newspaperman, for example, watched a bitter Virginia defeat at Chapel Hill and went home to write about the luxurious living of the Justices. While the rest of the student body, he wrote, sat in the stands dressed in modest, campus attire, Sarah Justice was smartly garbed in a new outfit which was crowned by a bright new hat. How many wives of other players could afford a fancy chapeau for a big game, he wondered.

The yarn brought a chuckle in the Justice household.

"See Sarah," Charlie told her, "that hat looks okay."

Sarah had worn the same hat from the very first game in 1946. The superstitious All-American wouldn't let her go to the stadium without it.

Charlie, himself, took most of the ribbing with rare good humor. He was especially apt when being interviewed and spoke with candor and a frankness that seldom was construed as cockiness. If a reporter asked a question, he got an answer.

113

The Justices and the Doak Walkers on parade

"You write it the way you want to," Justice always told the press. "I want to be truthful and give you the right answers. Sometimes they may not read well in print, and I'd appreciate it if you give me the benefit of the phrasing on that count."

He usually got more than a good press. It might be a column by Earle Hellen of the *Greensboro Record* one day, a profile for a national publication by Wilt Garrison of *The Charlotte Observer* the next. Larry Leonard of the *Richmond News Leader* always had an ear ready. Shelley Rolfe of the *Richmond Times-Dispatch* became embittered at the balloting procedure for the Heisman Trophy when Doak Walker edged Charlie one year, Leon Hart of Notre Dame, the next.

Only once or twice did Justice find himself on the wrong side of the reporting fraternity. One of these occasions came after he had completed his four years at Carolina. He attended a banquet at High Point and made a brief talk. The floor was opened for questions. A guest asked Justice if he felt Coach Wade at Duke was getting the most from his Blue Devils by utilizing the single wing.

"I feel," said Justice with no thought of being quoted, "that Coach Wade will probably have to make changes in their offensive structure to keep up with the terrific scoring trends of modern football."

The next day Charlie winced. Wire services carried a story saying, "JUSTICE CALLS WADE'S OFFENSE ANTIQUATED." The die-hards of Duke were burning. Columnists, who had been liberal in their adjectives for Justice as a schoolboy whiz, turned on him without offering him the chance for explanation. He was soundly censured as being a pop-off and a second-guesser.

"I made an apology to Coach Wade," said Charlie, "and I'm sure he realized I was offering no criticism of his coaching or his system. Coaches change their methods every season. That's all I meant by the statement. I wasn't misquoted. But a couple of more paragraphs to that original story would have saved me a lot of headaches."

While Justice was the leading individual in all four victories over Duke during the 1946-1949 picnic the Tar Heels were having at the expense of their old rival, Coach Wade seldom went on record in passing praise toward the tailback.

"I'd call it a good team win," Wade would usually say of Carolina's good fortune.

There were probably other reasons for the lack of verbosity on the part of the losing coach, but friends of Justice resented it. They didn't give consideration to the standing tradition of Wade to seldom single out individuals, even those of his own team. Wade was a firm believer in the player moulding himself to the team, not the team to the player.

"I never expected praise from Coach Wade," said Justice, "although I'll admit I'd have been happy to have read it. I always had the feeling he was bitter about my decision not to attend Duke.

"The story about my brother Jack not wanting me to play for him perhaps caused resentment. Jack simply felt my size was against me in a single wing attack

A lineup of sports celebrities includes sportscaster Harry Wismer (left), writer Hal Boyle, Justice, LeBaron, Graham and bandleader Tony Pastor.

based on power. He had nothing against Coach Wade as a man or as a coach. He was looking out for the shrimp of the family."

The shrimp of the Justice family was as durable as an oak knot. He seemed to be at the bottom of the pile in every play, yet he came up with a rhythm and a hustle that must have been disquieting for members of the opposition.

"I played with tough kids during my boyhood," said Charlie, "and I learned to hold the hurt inside . . . to never let anybody catch on. I also can thank my brothers for teaching me how to take a fall.

"That's most important for any successful back. The secret is in going as far as you can, then letting gravity take its course. Never brace—or some bones are sure to pop if a big guy decides to pile on for the fun of it.

"Injuries in football are usually the fault of the injured party. He's either loafing or thinking too much about what will happen to him. If a fellow puts out 100 per cent, he'll play a whale of a lot of football without too many serious bruises."

At times, as the Justice-led machines grew more prominent in national scope, there were rumors and rumblings that certain foes were "out to get the glamor boy."

No doubt, they were. No more than they were out to waylay Red Grange in his day, Bronko Nagurski in his day or Ace Parker in his moments of glory. It is the fate the super player must face.

"I can recall only a few times during my college career when I was really a 'target,'" Charlie would say. "Funny thing, but I always had my best success against players who were bent on injuring me. They thought more about what they were going to do to me when they got me, than they did in getting me. I found they faked pretty easy."

Justice suffered only a sprained ankle during his high school career, and was a college senior before he missed full time action at North Carolina. That was against Notre Dame—perhaps the one game he would have chosen to play above all others.

In pro ball, the wounds came with more frequency.

The number Justice wore at Carolina became as well known as the nickname of Choo Choo. The Post Office delivered letters each week simply addressed as "22," Chapel Hill, N. C.

Charlie earned his first "22" jersey in high school, but not until his junior year. As a sophomore under Coach Lee Stone at Lee Edwards High in Asheville, the narrow-shouldered hopeful took whatever number was available.

At Bainbridge, he switched numbers frequently.

Justice was always quick to praise the good coaching he received in high school, service and college. He was an extraordinary player, to be sure, but he was never a teacher's pet. He could take criticism and put it to use. A revealing document is a letter North Carolina's Snavely wrote the squad after the opening game against Georgia in 1947.

117

Charlie had the perfect target in Art Wiener

Snavely missives were famous for their outspokenness and thoroughness. The coach carefully researched films of the games and reported on each individual. Justice, who had been a leader in the win over the Bulldogs, rated almost a third of the comments. It was an abrupt changeover from the flattery he received in newspaper columns.

Wrote Snavely:

"It seems that no matter how thoroughly you practice, Charlie, you have difficulty in remembering in a game the things which are stressed on the practice field. One of the worst of your shortcomings in this respect is your failure to fake and to act. When you get in a game you are too interested in what the other boys are doing; you are governed too much by your impulses and not enough by good sound thinking.

"When you fail to fake properly you are laying down on the other backs who carry the ball and also on the whole team. You are not doing your share to advance the ball. The fact that you are tremendously interested in the play so that you must look back to see how it is coming along is no excuse for neglecting your part in it.

"We started the season emphasizing the principle that no fake was a fake unless it carried all the way across the line of scrimmage. You are not making any good pretense to take the ball when you do not take it; you look back; you let your hands drop; instead of running across the line of scrimmage, you take only a couple of steps and then you stop, and when you do this you can see the secondary men moving back toward the real runner and making it harder for our blockers to get them.

"On 163 you cut in once when you could have gone outside for a good gain. On 428-5 you should have cut back when the end started to cover you to the outside. On 129-3 you again failed to think as you executed the play. You ran much too far, you held the ball too long and then you stepped back and wound up. You stopped on 397. You looked back on 384. You made no fake to run on 129-4. You made no fake to run or to take the ball on 322-3. On 565, you once cut in when you could have gone for a touchdown on the outside, I believe.

"Charlie . . . these lapses of yours are serious."

Choo Choo was the star—but Snavely ran the stern shop of a perfectionist.

XIII

THEY SEARCHED FOR ADJECTIVES

He was Life magazine's cover boy.

"Choo Choo Spells Football," was the title of the yarn.

Commented Life: "A resident of Chapel Hill recently described Halfback Charlie Justice as the greatest Southerner since Robert E. Lee. Part of this adulation can be attributed to the sense of drama he brings to the game. When Justice goes back to receive a punt he somehow looks like a man who is going to run 60 or 70 yards for a touchdown. He often does."

Life said its piece well. Others searched for adjectives. There was so little time—and so much to write.

*   *   *   *   *   *

BILL CURRIE, a sportswriter turned broadcaster, wrote in the *High Point Enterprise*: "I never met a writer who didn't instantly like Charlie Justice. He's the only athlete I can recall with a daily press and a near spotless record."

It seemed that Charlie was destined to become everyone's champion. The young, the old, the literate and the unread sought to pat his back, to shake his hand and swell his importance.

One afternoon, after Charlie's college career had been concluded, a driver, sighting him walking down the street, doubleparked his automobile, dived out the door and yelled, "Choo Choo."

"Yessir," said Charlie, stopping and wondering about the urgency. The man rushed up, shook his hand and grabbed him by the shoulder.

"I just wanted to say hello and feel your muscles," he said with a grin. "You see, I never saw you play—but I listened to Jim Reid and Ray Reeve broadcast all the games on the radio. This is the first chance I've had to see you in person. It's a real thrill."

Jack Horner, of the *Durham Herald*, commented, "Justice is nothing less than the Red Grange of Southern football."

Added Chauncey Durden, of the *Richmond Times-Dispatch*: "Some will argue there have been better backs in the Southern Conference. Duke had a couple of good ones in Ace Parker and George McAfee . . . Clemson had Bonnie Banks McFadden. Virginia had Bill Dudley.

"But one thing no one will argue about: Justice's lure at the box office. The lithe, nervous Carolinian has packed every stadium he has played in. The Tar Heels were good enough to draw on their own, but Justice was the stadium-filler.

"Actually, Charlie was as much a favorite with non-Carolinians as he was with the Tar Heel rooting section. He possesses a magic that paid off in thrills and box office."

Justice can be linked with a trend in sports reporting that has become commonplace. That would be the personal interview with key players. While it was done to a limited extent before his appearance, most writers had been content to offer their own opinions and draw an occasional quote from the coaches.

The availability of Justice and the tremendous interest football fans had for his combat experiences found writers by the score visiting his dressing room. Editors soon found that if they didn't have a quote from Charlie the reader would seek another paper.

Dick Herbert, sports editor of the *Raleigh News and Observer*, made a trip to Dallas to compare for his readers the ability of Justice to that of Southern Methodist's Doak Walker. Frank Spencer, of the *Winston-Salem Journal*, dean of the Tar Heel writing tribe, wrote more about Charlie than any individual he covered in an illustrious career. Neale Patrick of Raleigh and Bill Cox of Norfolk were always in the press box, eager as freshmen in the stands.

Veteran reporters like Carlton Byrd, of the *Winston-Salem Sentinel*; Jack Willims, of the *Durham Herald*; Irwin Smallwood, of the *Greensboro News*, and Elton Casey, of the *Durham Sun*, smashed countless typewriter ribbons charting the Justice career. Wry Jake Penland, of the *Columbia (S. C.) State*, who enjoys feuds with everyone, found himself getting soft when he saw Choo Choo in action.

Charlie could do little wrong—whether he realized it or not.

A sermon was delivered one Sunday at the Baptist Church on Columbia Street in Chapel Hill. The title: "ALL THE WAY CHOO CHOO."

"When we call on Charlie Justice to go all the way," said the Rev. Dr. Samuel Tilden Habel, "we are placing a great responsibility on his shoulders—asking him to give everything, all his mind, his body, in going all the way."

120

A recent photo of Charlie on the sidelines with Assistant Coach Pat Pres

Baptist Church
SAMUEL TILDEN HABEL
MINISTER
9 45 CHURCH SCHOOL
11 MORNING WORSHIP
"ALL THE WAY,
CHOO CHOO"
6 PM STUDENT SUPPER

Then he called on his listeners to "go all the way in your work or profession and above all else go all the way in Christian living."

An interested listener was Charlie Justice.

In 1949, at the conclusion of the regular season, the Christian Athletes Foundation named Charlie recipient of its annual award. He was cited for "courage in the face of terrific physical punishment and unexpected defeat, for humility in the face of many honors, for loyalty to the church and for giving of time and interest to unfortunate children, for clean living and good sportsmanship in general."

The certificate meant as much to Charlie as the more elaborate cups, trophies, and fancier citations he had received from a hundred and one sources.

Coaches were liberal in their praise.

Articulate Art Guepe, a brilliant tactician at Virginia, paid Justice compliments at the slightest provocation.

"I admire Charlie," said Art, who had fallen to Justice's talents on three occasions, "and I always will. I consider him among the greatest backs of all time. By the way, that other fellow is a wizard, too."

He was speaking of Art Weiner, Charlie's All-American sidekick at end.

Frank Leahy, the Notre Dame coach, took time to write Justice after the 1949 game, which Charlie has squandered on the bench nursing an ankle wound.

Penned Leahy: "Just a note to let you know how sorry I am that you were unable to play against Notre Dame. I say this even though I know your presence would have caused the score to be different, because I know how much it would have meant for you to play in New York.

"I have long been one of your strongest admirers because when a young man can receive as much publicity as you have for four years and remain as level headed, he becomes a tremendous credit to intercollegiate football.

"Thus, every college football team in America has benefited by the marvelous representation you have made as a gentleman-athlete."

There were moments of not-so-serious comment on the fame of Charlie.

Hugo Germino, the saxophone-playing sports editor of the *Durham Sun*, happily noted one day a Durham restaurant offered as a main dish: "Choo Choo beef hash, Duke style."

While at Chapel Hill, Charlie and Sarah were given a handsome Boxer puppy which became known as "Choo Choo." The dog became a campus favorite and was permitted extra pleasures not known to Chapel Hill dogs since old, revered Dan expired during the war years. Charlie and "Choo Choo" created quite a familiar campus twosome.

The University-operated eating places were strict about animals, and spick-and span Lenoir Hall made it quite plain with a sign which admonished: "POSITIVELY NO DOGS ALLOWED."

A freshman, feeling rules were made to be broken, had scribbled underneath, ". . . EXCEPT CHOO CHOO'S."

Charlie didn't miss this sermon

Writing about Charlie wasn't confined to the sports pages. He even had his fans from Duke. An editorial in a North Carolina newspaper entitled "CHOO CHOO" offered:

"When a Duke graduate heaps praise upon a Carolina athlete, it is more of a news item than an editorial. Nevertheless, such is about to happen in this column.

"Charlie (Choo Choo) Justice goes down in our book as a swell guy, a good sport, a thrilling athlete and a valuable citizen. As his long and illustrious career comes to a close, the State of North Carolina can thank him for a lot of really good publicity, as well as many hours of exciting entertainment.

"A few young men have been known to be heroes on the football field, but their college and state preferred to mention them only in that one connection. Choo Choo, on the other hand, is a credit to the Tar Heel land in many ways."

If an athlete inspired a sermon, kept poets busy in composition, and drew more fan mail than some movie stars, it seemed inevitable a song should carry his exploits in a musical sense. Two bright young men, both friends of Justice, decided to do it—and turned out a hit that ranks with top college melodies of the past. They were Orville Campbell (Mr. Words) and Hank Beebe (Mr. Music).

Benny Goodman, the famed jazz clarinetist, and Johnny Long, a Duke grad who plays a violin from the port side, were among the top recording artists who found "All the Way . . ." worth their time.

Smith Barrier, of the *Greensboro News*, interpreted the ditty for his readers in this manner:

"Try the verses for size:

"A two-ton tackle got his man; across him laid his two-ton span.
"'Don't move,' Two Ton said to him, 'Choo Choo may come back again.'"

(This goes back to the '48 Duke game, which was 0 to 0 until Choo Choo went 48 yards on his most amazing maneuver of the year. Tackle Ted Hazlewood, while blocking, is said to have quipped to his Duke opponent as Charlie was cutting back and forth, "Don't move, Choo Choo may come by here several more times.")

"A touchdown pass would break a tie; the end said, 'Hit me in the eye.'
"While thousands roared the coach looked glum; Choo Choo merely said,
'Which one?'"

(Choo Choo's pitching mark that '48 season was 62 completions for 122 throws —good for 838 yards and 12 touchdowns.)

"Punt formation once was called; Choo Choo waited for the ball.
"Why it ought to be against the law; they found that thing in Ark-an-saw."

(It refers to Charlie's remarkable average—and one kick in particular against Maryland when the pigskin traveled 84 yards from the line of scrimmage.)

125

A word of advice from Coach Joe Kuharich of Washington

> *"At the football games he does all the stunts; he runs, he passes, fakes or*
> *punts.*
> *"Between the halves he leads the band; then sells peanuts in the stands."*

The chorus, which had a solid beat that collegians could appreciate and words easy to remember and repeat, went:

> *All the way Choo Choo, all the way;*
> *A chug, chug, chugga with a hip hooray.*
> *Bing, bat, boot that ball around;*
> *Open that throttle and cover ground.*

The song sold 32,000 copies.

Charles Ronald Justice was born August 23, 1949, and the Justices decided to call him Ronnie. "I hope no one ever decides to brand him 'Little Choo Choo,'" sighed Charlie.

When the youngster was four days old, Roy Armstrong, then Carolina's director of admissions, sent an official application blank in care of his parents with this note:

"Dear Ronnie:

"I want to welcome you to Chapel Hill and congratulate your mother and father on the fine job they have done.

"As you know, colleges are quite crowded today. Therefore, I feel you should lose no time in returning the enclosed form.

"I want to caution you not to sign anything where you are now living (Duke Hospital) because we want no question raised as to your eligibility, nor do we want it said that the University of North Carolina has used any inducements or encouragements to lead you away from any neighboring institutions."

The appearance of Ronnie on the scene stirred young Billy Carmichael III, sports editor of *The Daily Tar Heel* and an outspoken champion of Choo Choo during his collegiate career, to write an "open letter" to the tyke. It pleased Charlie greatly and read in part:

"Dear Ronnie:

"You see, Ronnie, though you have been born into the Hall of Justice, there is one privilege you probably never can be afforded—that of seeing your father play football at Carolina.

"Your father became more than a football player, Ronnie. He was a fable, a legend and a reality all rolled into one.

"Your daddy, Ronnie, lived and played hard and from his heart. He hated to lose, for in defeat he felt only his own failures. He played the game to win—and usually did."

127

They came, young and old, for autographs and handshakes

Open letters seemed to be in vogue. Another one was drafted over the wires of the *Associated Press* the week before Charlie played his final game at Kenan Stadium. The author was Ken Alyta of Charlotte, the *AP's* sports chief:

"Dear Charlie:

"Since I won't be making the Virginia game this week, the Carolina-Duke game last Saturday marked for me, at least, the last chance to see you play college football.

"I just thought I ought to tell you how much I've enjoyed watching you this year and last and thank you for the thrilling afternoons of football you've given me.

"You see, being a Connecticut carpetbagger I could watch your play in more or less a detached manner without the emotional stress and strain of an old grad trying hard to be impartial.

"I saw you and Carolina eight times, beginning last fall with that breathtaking Texas game. You always won. Somehow I escaped the pitfalls of your seasons.

"I've admired the way in which you've stood up under pressure. It was terrific for three years, but this fall you were expected to combine the better features of Frank Merriwell and Superman week after week. Usually you did.

"You've been given the full treatment a la Hollywood the past three months. You've kept your head, refused to cry over the bad breaks and kept pitching. You've been All-America off the field as well as on.

"Just thought I ought to let you know. So long, Charlie, it's been wonderful watching you."

Alyta was speaking for hundreds of fans and writers and disciples of the Justice era. But even his sincere and flattering sendoff failed to convey the feeling youngsters had for Charlie. An impromptu election at a classroom of an orphanage in North Carolina told the real story.

A teacher asked his pupils to write on a slip of paper the most important man in the country. Twenty-six slips were passed out, marked and returned.

The principal of the institution received one vote.

The President of the United States, Harry Truman, received two.

The other 23 went to Charlie (Choo Choo) Justice.

CHOO CHOO'S TIMETABLE
Charlie Justice's Year-By-Year Totals

1946 (8-2-1, Including Sugar Bowl)

RUSHING: Carried 149 times, gained 1061 yards, lost 81 yards, net gain 980 yards

PASSING: Attempted 53, completed 20, had 10 intercepted, net gain 275 yards, 1 touchdown

TOTAL OFFENSE: 202 plays, 1255 yards

PASS RECEIVING: Received 2, gained 39 yards, scored one touchdown

PUNTING: Kicked 51 times, 2092 yards, averaged 41.0 yards, two blocked

PUNT RETURNS: Returned 19, 228 yards

KICKOFF RETURNS: Returned 11, 391 yards

TOUCHDOWNS: 12 scored, 72 points

1947 (8-2-0)

RUSHING: Carried 125 times, gained 672 yards, lost 124, net gain 548 yards

PASSING: Attempted 50, completed 27, had 5 intercepted, net gain 382 yards, 6 touchdowns

TOTAL OFFENSE: 175 plays, 930 net yards gained

PASS RECEIVING: Received 6, gained 119 yards, scored three touchdowns

INTERCEPTION RETURNS: Intercepted two, returned 23 yards

PUNTING: Kicked 61 times, 2538 yards, 41.6 yards average, none blocked

PUNT RETURNS: Returned 24, returned 283 yards

KICKOFF RETURNS: Returned seven, returned 156 yards

SCORING: Eight touchdowns scored, 48 points

1948 (9-1-1, Including Sugar Bowl)

RUSHING: Carried 163, gained 968, lost 118, net gain 850

PASSING: Attempted 135, completed 68, had 12 intercepted, net gain 911 yards, 12 touchdowns

TOTAL OFFENSE: 298 plays, 1761 yards gained

PASS RECEIVING: Received four passes, gained 46 yards, scored one touchdown

INTERCEPTION RETURNS: Intercepted one pass, returned 10 yards

PUNTING: Kicked 70 times, 3032 yards, average 44.0 (new National record compiled regular season. Punting for 11 games, including Sugar Bowl, dropped to 43.7 yards per kick.)

PUNT RETURNS: Returned 24, 566 yards

KICKOFF RETURNS: Returned six, 161 yards

TOUCHDOWNS: 11 touchdowns scored, 66 points

1949 (7-4-0, Including Cotton Bowl) (Captain)

RUSHING: Carried 139 times, gained 573 yards, lost 137, net gain 436 yards

PASSING: Attempted 113, completed 58, had seven intercepted, net gain 794, scored 6 touchdowns

TOTAL OFFENSE: 252 plays, 1230 yards

PASS RECEIVING: Caught 7, gained 36 yards, scored one touchdown

INTERCEPTION RETURNS: None

PUNTING: Kicked 69 times, 3007 yards, average 43.6, none blocked

PUNT RETURNS: Returned 7, 123 yards

KICKOFF RETURNS: Returned 10, 201 yards

TOUCHDOWNS: Scored 8 touchdowns, 48 points

Four-Year Totals

RUSHING: Carried 576 times, gained 3274 yards, lost 460 yards, net 2814 yards, average gain 4.9 yards per try

PASSING: Attempted 351, completed 173, had 34 intercepted, gained 2362 yards, 26 scoring passes, percentage .493

TOTAL OFFENSE: 927 plays, 5176 yards gained, average 5.6 yards (new NCAA record)

PASS RECEIVING: Caught 19, gained 240 yards, scored 6 touchdowns

INTERCEPTION RETURNS: Intercepted 3 passes, returned 33 yards

PUNTING: (New NCAA record) kicked 251 times, 10,669 yards, average 42.5, 2 blocked

PUNT RETURNS: Returned 74, 1200 yards, average return 16.2 yards

KICKOFF RETURNS: Returned 34, 909 yards, average return 26.7 yards

SCORING: 39 touchdowns, 234 points

BOWL GAME LINEUPS

SUGAR BOWL—JANUARY 1, 1947

NORTH CAROLINA	GEORGIA
LE—Romano, Powell, Tandy	LE—Tereshinski, Moseley
LT—Williamson, Fowle, Jarrell	LT—Williams, Jenkins
LG—Strayhorn, Mitten, Cheek	LG—St. John, Payne
C—Weant, Steigman	C—Cooley, Deavers, Chandler
RG—Varney, Roberts, Spurlin	RG—George, Alexander
RT—Szafaryn, Hazlewood, Marczyk	RT—Bush, Perhach
RE—Sparger, Cox, Rubish, Logue	RE—Edwards, Sellers
QB—Wright, Sutherland, Hartig	QB—Rauch
LH—Justice, Maceyko	LH—Smith, Donaldson, Maricich
RH—Camp, Clements, Fitch, Grow	RH—Trippi, Jernigan
FB—Pupa, Rodgers	FB—McPhee, Geri

UNC	0	7	3	0—10
Georgia	0	0	13	7—20

UNC scoring: Touchdowns—Pupa; field goal—Cox. Georgia: Touchdowns—Rauch 2, Edwards; point after touchdown—Jernigan 2.

SUGAR BOWL—JANUARY 1, 1949

NORTH CAROLINA	OKLAHOMA
LE—Weiner, Powell, Romano	LE—Tipps, Owens
LT—Highsmith, Fowle	LT—Paine, Manley
LG—Mitten, Wardle	LG—Burris, McNabb
C—Steigman, Holdash	C—Tillman, Powell, Bodenhamer
RG—Varney, Klosterman	RG—Mayes, Andros, West
RT—Hazlewood, Szafaryn	RT—Walker, Trotter
RE—Cox, Rubish, Cooke	RE—Goad, Anderson
QB—Knox, Rizzo	QB—Lisak, Mitchell
LH—Justice, Maceyko, Purcell	LH—Royal, Pearsons
RH—Kennedy, Clements	RH—Jones, Thomas, Brewer
FB—Rodgers, Weant	FB—Greathouse, Heath, Ming

UNC	6	0	0	0— 6
Oklahoma	7	0	7	0—14

UNC scoring: Touchdowns—Rodgers. Oklahoma: Touchdowns—Mitchell, Pearsons; point after touchdown—Ming 2.

COTTON BOWL—JANUARY 2, 1950

NORTH CAROLINA	RICE
LE—Weiner, Nickerson, O'Brien	LE—J. Williams, Allen, Broughton, Howton
LT—King, Wiley, Rywak, Carpenter	LT—Anderson, Wyman, Walls
LG—Bestwick, Hansen, McDonald, Wardle	LG—Roberts, Derwood, Lee, McPhail, Meumann
C—Holdash, Miketa	C—Watson, Weatherly, Stonestreet, Price
RG—Augustine, Dudeck, Woodell	RG—Schwarz, Delwood, Lee
RT—Kuhn, Ruffin, Williams, Hendrick	RT—Murphy, Geroski, Winship
RE—Powell, Washington, Bilpuch, Kelso	RE—Taylor, McCurry, Pugh
QB—Knox, Rizzo, Kosinski	QB—Riley, Rote, Glass, Carswell
LH—Justice, Bunting, Curtis	LH—Wyatt, Silver
RH—Carson, Clements, Verchick, Norcross, Dougherty	RH—Burkhalter, Proctor, Kelly
FB—Weiss, Gantt, Hayes, Stevens, Hesmer	FB—Lantrip, Glauser

UNC	0	0	0	13—13
Rice	0	14	7	6—27

UNC scoring: Touchdowns—Rizzo 2; point after touchdown—Williams. Rice: Touchdowns—Burkhalter 2, Lantrip, Williams; point after touchdown—J. Williams 3.

130

CAROLINA-DUKE LINEUPS

NOVEMBER 23, 1946

NORTH CAROLINA	DUKE
LE—Romano, Tandy	LE—Mote, Gantt
LT—Jarrell, Fowle, Williamson	LT—Allen, Mullins
LG—Strayhorn, Mitten, Cheek	LG—Milner, B. Davis
C—Highsmith, Steigman	C—Wall, Bethune, Perkinson
RG—Varney, Roberts, Spurlin, McDonald	RG—Knotts, Chambers
RT—Szafaryn, Plunkett, Marczyk	RT—DeRogatis, Oenbrink
RE—Sparger, Rubish, Cox	RE—Smith, Citadino
QB—Wright, Hartig	QB—Montgomery, Eslick, Straus
LH—Justice, Myers, Maceyko	LH—Clark, Folger, H. Hartley, B. Hartley
RH—Camp, Clements, Fitch, Grow	RH—Mulligan, Luper, Williams
FB—Pupa, Rodgers	FB—Long, Inman

UNC	0	7	0	15—22
Duke	0	7	0	0— 7

UNC scoring: Touchdowns—Justice, Fitch, Tandy, (plus safety). Duke: Touchdown—Long; point after touchdown—B. Hartley.

NOVEMBER 22, 1947

NORTH CAROLINA	DUKE
LE—Powell, Weiner, Romano, Logue	LE—Cittadino, Hardison, Duncan
LT—Fowle, Smith	LT—Allen, DeRogatis
LG—Wardle, Cheek	LG—Chambers, Wall
C—Sparger	C—Gleason
RG—Roberts, Mitten, Klosterman	RG—Davis, Karmazin
RT—Szafaryn	RT—Eisenberg, Reese, Gardner
RE—Rubish, Cox, Cooke, Tandy, Pritchard	RE—Austin, Lyle
QB—Wright, Weant, Knox, Hartig	QB—Montgomery, Eslick
LH—Maceyko, Justice	LH—Folger, Herlong
RH—Clements, Camp, Sherman, Fitch	RH—Clark, Hughes, Williams, Mulligan, Hodges
FB—Pupa, Hayes, Flamish, Kennedy	FB—Hartley, Stephanz, Viau, Swalchick

UNC	0	12	9	0—21
Duke	0	0	0	0— 0

UNC scoring: Touchdowns—Justice 2, Cox; field goal—Cox.

NOVEMBER 21, 1948

NORTH CAROLINA	DUKE
LE—Weiner, Romano, Powell	LE—Duncan, Souchak, Heise
LT—Fowle, Highsmith, Marczyk, Cospito	LT—Allen, Reese, Young
LG—Wardle, Mitten	LG—Knotts, Marshall, Sherrill
C—Neikirk, Holdash, Steigman	C—Perkinson, Karmazin, Harris
RG—Varney, Klosterman	RG—Davis, Karl
RT—Szafaryn, Hazlewood	RT—DeRogatis, Eisenberg, Anderson
RE—Cox, Cooke, Rubish	RE—Austin, Bryant, Lyons
QB—Weant, Knox, Rizzo	QB—Montgomery, Eslick, Harris
LH—Maceyko, Justice, Purcell	LH—Folger, Cox, Frye
RH—Clements, Kennedy, Bunting	RH—Friedlund, Brown, Hughes
FB—Rodgers	FB—Stephanz, Mounie, Viau

UNC	0	0	6	14—20
Duke	0	0	0	0— 0

UNC scoring: Touchdowns—Weiner 2, Justice; point after touchdown—Cox 2.

NOVEMBER 20, 1949

NORTH CAROLINA	DUKE
LE—Nickerson, Weiner, Bledsoe, O'Brien	LE—Souchak, Youmans, Earon
LT—Rywak, King, Hansen, Carpenter, Wiley	LT—Allen, Young, Eisenberg
LG—McDonald, Wardle, Bestwick	LG—Chambers, Cavanaugh, Knotts
C—Neikirk, Holdash, Stevens	C—J. E. Gibson, Viau, Perkinson
RG—Dudeck, Augustine, Hord, Slate	RG—James, Karl, Sherrill
RT—Kuhn, Hendrick, Ruffin, Williams	RT—Reese, Anderson
RE—Bilpuch, Powell, Washington, Kelso	RE—Hughes, Bryant, Heiss, J. F. Gibson
QB—Knox, Rizzo	QB—Hager, Skipworth, Stephanz
LH—Bunting, Justice, Hesmer, Carson, Page	LH—Cox, Wild
RH—Clements, Gantt, Verchick	RH—Friedlund, Schoonmaker, Brown
FB—Wiess, Hayes, Curtis	FB—Powers, Self, Higgins

UNC	0	7	14	0—21
Duke	6	0	7	7—20

UNC scoring: Touchdowns—Weiner 2, Justice; safety—Wiley (blocked punt); point after touchdown—Williams. Duke: Touchdowns—Cox 2, Powers; point after touchdown—Souchak 2.

U.N.C. ALL-AMERICANS

George Barclay (Guard)	Associated Press (1934) All-America Board (1934) Williamson (1934)
Andy Bershak (End)	G. Rice, Collier's (1937) NEA (1937) Williamson (1937)
Steve Maronic (Tackle)	Central Press (1938) Liberty (1938)
Paul Severin (End)	Associated Press (1939) Associated Press (1940)
Charlie Justice (Halfback)	Collier's (1948, 1949) Associated Press (1948, 1949) United Press (1948) All-America Board (1948) Sport Magazine (1948, 1949) Williamson (1948, 1949) Paramount (1948, 1949) Bill Stern (1948, 1949) Int. News Service (1948)
Art Weiner (End)	G. Rice, Look (1948) N. Y. Daily News (1949) New York Sun (1949)
Ken Powell (End)	Williamson (1949) NEA (1949)
Irvin Holdash (Center)	NEA (1950) Williamson (1950)

132

This book was set in 12 point Garamond. The paper is Mead's Black and White Enamel and the book was printed by Colonial Press of Chapel Hill, North Carolina. The book was bound by Carolina Ruling and Binding, Charlotte. Lawrence Campbell was in charge of design and production. The photographs, unless otherwise noted, are by Hugh Morton.